FISHING WITH MY FATHERS

FISHING
WITH MY
FATHERS

PAUL D. RATH

WOOD LAKE

Editor: Mike Schwartzentruber
Proofreader: Dianne Greenslade
Design: Robert MacDonald

Library and Archives Canada Cataloguing in Publication
Title: Fishing with my fathers / Paul D. Rath.
Names: Rath, Paul D., 1957- author.
Identifiers: Canadiana (print) 20200399136 | Canadiana (ebook) 20200399349 |
ISBN 9781773434087 (softcover) | ISBN 9781773434094 (HTML)
Subjects: LCSH: Rath, Paul D., 1957- – Family. | LCSH: Fathers and sons – British
Columbia – Okanagan Lake – Biography. | LCSH: Fishing – British Columbia –
Okanagan Lake. | LCSH: Okanagan Lake (B.C.) – Biography. | LCGFT:
Autobiographies.
Classification: LCC SH572.B8 R38 2021 | DDC 799.1092 – dc23

ISBN 978-1-77343-408-7

Published by Wood Lake Publishing Inc.
485 Beaver Lake Road, Kelowna, BC, Canada, V4V 1S5
www.woodlake.com | 250.766.2778

Wood Lake Publishing acknowledges the financial support of the Government
of Canada. Wood Lake Publishing acknowledges the financial support of the
Province of British Columbia through the Book Publishing Tax Credit.

Wood Lake Publishing would like to acknowledge that we operate in the
unceded territory of the Syilx/Okanagan People, and we work to support
reconciliation and challenge the legacies of colonialism. The Syilx/Okanagan
territory is a diverse and beautiful landscape of deserts and lakes, alpine
forests and endangered grasslands. We honour the ancestral stewardship of
the Syilx/Okanagan People.

Printed in Canada.
Printing 10 9 8 7 6 5 4 3 2 1

CONTENTS

The old drunk told me about trout fishing.
When he could talk, he had a way of describing trout
– as if they were a precious and intelligent metal.

– Richard Brautigan, *Trout Fishing in America*

This book is dedicated to

the Reverend Ernest Rath –
my pastor,
my father,
my friend and fishing buddy.

And to my grandson George,
to help him know his great-grandfather,
and better understand his grandfather,
and his place in the tapestry
of our family.

GOOD COMPANY

An Introduction

I started this book by writing a poem, many years ago, back when I thought the way out of being a pastor, like my father, was to be a poet, like e. e. cummings. For years I wrote playful poems. Twenty years after Brazilian poets stopped writing concrete poetry, I tried unsuccessfully to revive the revolution and bring it to Canada. The reception was cool. I sought solace in fishing. Then, one day, shivers went down my spine as I wrote this:

> In November,
> the wind takes us into her cold mouth,
> and crunches us between her teeth.
> Her cold makes our eyes freeze –
> until they feel like stones,
> frozen in their sockets of mud.
> Our cheeks burn,
> as we stand on the ice-glazed rocks,
> with twelve feet of bamboo pole,
> thirteen feet of 40-pound test line,
> and a red teardrop hook,
> baited with a maggot or two.
>
> Between fish,
> my father and I,
> two men who are as comfortable
> with each other's voice as we are with each other's silences,
> talk about the purpose of things,
> and how everything fits
> into the overall design.

Rocks, trees, clouds, people
all have a purpose,
a place in the Master Plan.
We know maggots are useful,
as we push them onto the hook.
Maggots are the secret to white fishing.

Suckers on the other hand
are not useful.
You can't eat them – or could –
but wouldn't want to,
unless you were starving.
Suckers also eat maggots
and clean off your hook
so the white fish won't bite,
and if you accidentally hook a sucker
their weight can snap the bamboo pole in half
and shorten your fishing trip.

One time
a sucker broke my father's pole
and he waded into
the icy water
up to his waist
to retrieve it.
He spent the rest of the trip
shivering in the car
with the heat turned up full blast.

We are silent for a minute,
content with ourselves,
content with our place in the scheme of things,
happy with each other,

glad to be in the cold wind,
pondering quietly
the reason for suckers
in the lake of life.

And Mom thinks we come out here
for the fish.

After another 20 years, I thought it was probably best to take you fishing with us, what with Dad being gone and Mom in a home, with her memories tangled. It's no good fishing alone.

A real conversation about life, death, and forgiveness – that's the thing you need out here on the edge of the water.

As much as this book may be about fishing, it is even more about relationships. It explores the physical relationship and love of a father for his son and of a son for his father. It is also about the spiritual relationship between a pastor and a member of his flock that is further complicated by the fact that the pastor is also the father. It is also about my spiritual relationship with my heavenly Father.

As the son of a Lutheran pastor who spent 40 years in the ministry (six of those as a missionary in Brazil), I was both son and parishioner. I saw my father's triumphs and frustrations first-hand. Often, I was the cause of both ends of that emotional spectrum. As his son, I felt the need to challenge his authority and to test the extent and depth of his faith. As my father, he was resolved to put the "word of God" into my hands and to guide me towards regular attendance at church. As my pastor, he tried to help me make God-pleasing choices in my life, how to be less angry and vengeful and more forgiving. Sometimes the lines between our roles were blurred. Sometimes I would not accept a lesson from my father that I would accept from my pastor, and vice versa. Some lessons are more easily learned with a fishing rod in your hand.

One thing we had in common on this complicated journey together was fishing. I thought if I went fishing with him, it would guarantee that he would take a day off and find some respite from his stress. He felt that if he went fishing with me, he would have another chance to illustrate the benefits of kindness, compassion, generosity, and forgiveness. These lessons could also be passed on to my children. He hoped. These lessons, which my father is still trying to teach me today, are slowly sinking in.

I was not one to burn bridges. Not because I was smart enough to realize that if I burned the bridge there would be no way back across the river should I need to do that in the future, but because burning bridges was not my style. I was more about dropping a nuclear device on the bridge, so that no one, including myself, could cross there for 10,000 years. Not smart, but predictable.

Some lessons took hold better than others. As we stood together on the shores of Okanagan Lake, we hooked onto some of the big questions. What was our purpose in life? What happens after you die? How do you forgive someone who has wronged you? Some of Jesus' disciples were fishermen, so we were in good company.

I witnessed how leprosy, which my father caught in Brazil and which caused him excruciating pain, deepened him, and gave him a profound ability to relate to those who were dying or in pain. It reminded me of Romans 8:28. "We know that all things work together for good for those who love God, who are called according to his purpose" (NRSV).

That's how I came to understand how leprosy affected my father's ability to fish. I learned where I fit into the mosaic of Raths that had come before and, by extension, where I might fit in with those who might eventually follow. I am a conduit, a bridge between my great-grandfather George, and my grandson, also named George.

I am not a preacher, like my father. Your soul is not my primary concern. Some will say that I sound like a preacher, I admit that. Understand that it is not deliberate. There was a time when I felt the call to ministry, or thought I did, but that is another story altogether. If, however, you have an open mind, are willing to leave the warmth of your bed long before the return of the sun is even hinted at, willing to drive for an hour and then walk in the crisp November air, in near darkness, to stand on the rocks at first light, bracing yourself against the icy wind, I can teach you how to catch white fish. It won't be easy, and I am not a patient teacher, but there are rewards, and they are many.

This book is about recognizing the goodness of God in the strength of a father-son relationship and in the beauty of the world. God created the abundance. God provides. God engineered white fish to come like clockwork to the rocky shores of Okanagan Lake. This is my tribute to my father, and my pastor.

The actual advice on how to catch white fish is also practical and sound.

THE NOVICE

THE SECRET TO CATCHING WHITE FISH

To succeed at white fishing, forget what you know. You may have caught salmon off the coast of British Columbia. For that, consider yourself fortunate. But even if your salmon knowledge is broad and your experience extensive, it is of no value on the lake.

You may have fished off the coast of Costa Rica, with dolphins swimming around you as far as the horizon, in every direction – a dizzying circus of movement. You were, no doubt, thrilled as a sailfish leaped from the water, trying to shake your hook in the vastness of the ocean, out of the sight of land. I bet your heart was beating as fast as a hummingbird's wings. You probably have video. Impressive. That doesn't, however, translate into catching white fish.

You may have fished jackfish and pickerel in Georgian Bay on Lake Huron, with its scrubby, windblown trees and rocky islands straight out of a painting by the Group of Seven. But that has nothing to do with fishing for white fish, because fishing for white fish is an art of its own.

To fish for white fish, you have to be present in the moment you are living right now. If I tell you (for instance), to clear your mind and focus on the float (and I'm about to), I would not be trying to convert you to Buddhism, which I might be if I told you to become "one with the float." I'd never say that. What I'm doing is telling you the secret of how to catch white fish, how to block out everything that is *not* the float.

Michelangelo once said that the process of creating a sculpture was to remove everything that was not part of the sculpture. It is the same with white fishing. Strip yourself and the world down until the entire universe is your float and you are in orbit around your float, with the gravitational pull of the Earth keeping your attention there, and only there. If you lose your concentration even for a second, you will burn up like a meteor. Focus. Have you ever seen the bottom of a lake? Probably not. Yet you have probably experienced the depth of a lake. That's what you're doing here. Your task is to explore beneath the waves, into the unseen realm, without using your eyes, your ears, or your arms.

Do not try to peer beneath the waves! Your eyes will report only a distorted, magnified, and unrealistic view. Don't let yourself be lured there. You are a blind man, feeling your way through the world, exploring the lake bottom with your float. Trust only your float. The float is your eyes and your ears. It is your probe and your tether, your lifeline into what you cannot see. It doesn't matter that it is not touching the bottom. It is there, anyway, exploring hidden mysteries.

So clear your mind. Chip off anything that is not a fluorescent orange float riding on the water. It races along the top of the waves like a sailboat. It is tethered to you by 40-pound test line, which is the only thing strong enough to withstand the cold. The line is attached to the rod. It telegraphs information to your arm, which sends its vibrations to your brain.

The hard part is chipping away at distractions. It requires discipline not to look at the clouds, or the mountains, or the traffic on the road, or the rocks, or at Joe taking another fish off the hook; or even inside your head to Jesus fishing for men on the Sea of Galilee, or at memories of your father picking up hitchhikers so that he can ask them about their relationship with God at 50 mph and telephone poles gliding past. Be on the water, weightless, a float, which is a little thing – floating, out there, so far you can hardly feel it. It is your heart. That is your heart out there, floating.

You are learning to speak float language. You are able to tell immediately if your line is tangled, if you are touching bottom, if your hook is no longer moving in the correct area, working the arc with the wind. The magical arc reaches from "ten o'clock" to "two o'clock" – or from "two" to "ten" depending on the direction of the wind. If you fish at nine o'clock, or at "three," your float is no longer moving through optimal water. You are wasting your time, fishing dead water. Keep your float moving like a metronome. It is a scythe. Find the rhythm. Work the wind.

There are many other secrets to catching white fish. None are about fish. Sure, I can teach you how to bait a hook, how to tie various knots, how to cast against a brisk wind and use it to your advantage, but I cannot teach you how to calm your mind, how to clear your mind of everything that is not this float, on this water, at this time. That you must learn how to do yourself, and if you think it'll be easy, remember this: thinking about other days, other floats, and other water, are merely distractions. What matters is this float, this water under this float, right now, and not even the fish approaching your hook.

The float is your life, nothing else. The cold November wind cannot be allowed to distract you, not even for a second. Your unpaid bills or an argument with your boss must be left behind. The snowflakes that kiss your cheeks and the frozen pellets of ice driven against your skin, must be ignored. The float is the crux of the matter, the fulcrum that connects the hook by fishline to your rod, from your rod to your arm, and from your arm to the breathing apparatus that keeps you asleep nights, so you don't wake up gasping like a fish out of water, choking on breath that is not there.

Fishing for white fish is not even about catching or eating fish. It is about denying the physical needs of the body to explore the unknown. The surface of the water is a membrane that separates one realm from another, just like your diaphragm separates your internal organs from your heart and lungs.

I know about this. I have a hiatus hernia, which is a weakness in my diaphragm. At times, my guts want to come up into my chest cavity. This experience mimics having a heart attack: lots of pressure, burning pain, and the potential of passing through the veil. That is exactly what you don't want to be thinking about.

Singers use the power of the diaphragm to project their voices.

White fishers explore the realm beneath the waves and think about leaving this body.

A new fisherman will react more quickly but lacks experience. An experienced fisherman who has learned to speak float will out-fish the novice. On the other hand, the experienced fisherman never knows when his last trip to the Rock might be and comes away with more questions than answers. He never really gets any answers, but sometimes there are fish. They pierce the veil.

Focusing on the float is a difficult and complex task. The rod tip has to be up, and the line taut. If there is too much slack in your line, you won't be able to hook the fish because you're going to waste precious time getting the slack out. By then the fish will be gone. On the other hand, if your line is too taut, the float won't lie on the water right and will give you false alarms.

It is not enough to just *observe* the float. You have to interpret its clues and be prepared to act in a split second. If you are standing close to the water and the wind is pushing the waves from the south, you need to know the difference between a regular wave that will not get you wet, and the big one that could sweep you off your rocky perch. Part of you needs to monitor the wave action as you focus on your float. Often a bite will come when the float encounters the wave. You need to anticipate this event and to be ready.

The relaxation comes from the focus. Time ceases to exist. There is just you, the float, the line, the rod, and the approaching wave. There is no time to consider the beauty of the spot you are in, or how the clouds appear to be moving above you. There is no time to think about your mortgage or where your grocery money is coming from this week. The whole universe is distilled down to just you and the float. You are floating. That's all there is to it.

Actually, fishing for white fish is not really about the float. That is an illusion you maintain so you can spend time with your father, who is maintaining his own illusions so he can spend time with you. Somehow, he has identified you as the son who needs to learn about floating on water, *not* the son, the younger one, who needs to learn about floating on air, and who gets time alone with him and with kites and string.

The fish we are catching have come to spawn. The does are bursting with roe, and the bucks are bursting with milt. Some of each ends up in the pail, along with the fish. One of my last tasks before leaving the Rock was to pour the roe and milt mixture that had collected in the pail back into the lake. Perhaps, by some miracle, I contributed in a small way to the spawning process that was taking place.

I hope so.

HOW TO TELL TIME LIKE A FISHERMAN

When the water is blue in November – the striking innocent blue of a blue-eyed baby, the bottomless blue you have come to expect of Okanagan Lake, the mighty blue of summer fun, tourists, and heat – you know something is wrong. The unseasonal deep blue of summer against the dark mountain peaks of Okanagan Mountain Park that lie like a sleeping dragon, nose pointed west across from you, will likely show snow amid the sparse trees. You can almost hear the elk bugling for a mate in the frosty air. Almost. The elk are there because, for the most part, the park is inaccessible.

This kind of blue does not belong in November and means that there is too much light, too much sky in the water, and that the fish will stay in the darker water just beyond your reach. Clouds will be reflected in blue water, and you will be distracted from your float. You will want to remember how the clouds float on the mirrored surface in front of you, just because of the beauty of it, but this is a trap. Do not fall for it. Your float is still because there is no wind. You will lift your gaze to the wisps of cloud that cling like cotton to the tree whiskers on the mountain peaks, and just then, when your attention is taken away for a second, a bite will come and you will miss it. Stop, rein yourself in. Thoughts like these will not produce any fish.

The water is not always blue. Sometimes it is grey. Not the grey of mist or cloud, not even the grey of cloud heavy with rain; but colder, darker, the colour of wet slate, with a smell like wet wool mixed with seaweed and fish. It is the colour of the North Atlantic in a winter gale, when in your darkest hour you fear that all colour and even the love of God have abandoned you. It is the colour of the sea-stained granite rocks at Peggy's Cove, where posted signs warn you to keep off the dark rocks lest a rogue wave pluck you off and carry you out to sea. It is the colour of the Tomb of the Unknown Soldier. It is the colour of acid rain.

Optimal conditions are when the grey of the water and the grey of the sky are one. If it is almost impossible to tell where one ends and the other begins, the fish will feel comfortable enough to be in the shallows. When all colour has been absorbed, neutralized, as if colour were made illegal by some daft bureaucrat, or taxed mercilessly; when all the colour has gone underground and you can barely remember a rainbow, the fish will come.

Good wave action means having waves that are pushed by a wind from the south to crash unimpeded into Antlers Beach like rollers on the ocean. As soon as you step out of the car, you can hear the roar of the waves as they meet the shore. What you don't know is how the waves will be at the Rock, a mile to the south. Will they be crashing over the Rock, trying to sweep you off, or soaking you to the skin? Will the waves be manageable?

The worst is when you get out of the car and the lake is flat and calm, without a swell at all. Hope for wind then, to give the waves a push, so your hook can dance beneath the waves and attract the fish, distracting them from their primary purpose, which is to find a mate and propagate.

In optimal fishing weather, the water might be the dark grey of tombstones, but is alive, each swell a heartbeat. If the wind is steady from the south, swells break across the Rock from right to left. The water slaps against stone, and from some unseen chamber beneath your feet you can hear small stones chuckling, and the hollow thud of water being forced into a dead-end chute.

Not all swells are the same size. Some say that every seventh wave is larger. You don't have time to count, but you need to be aware of the roar of the waves as they approach – and be ready to jump to higher ground when a cleansing wave covers the Rock with a foot of icy water.

The wind is necessary to push the waves, though. A steady wind is workable. If the wind gets unruly, you can still place your float in the right spot, but it is harder. The wind pelts your cheeks with snow and frozen bits of ice. Try to take no notice. Cast against the wind and use it to move your float in an arc through the optimal fishing zone.

Water, waves, and wind are the trinity of white fishing. You need to know this by heart. You don't think about breathing, or beating your heart, or blinking your eyes – each of these things happens unconsciously. Fishing for white fish is like that. While you are focusing on your float, be aware on a deeper level of the water, waves, and wind. Allow your subconscious to handle those details so you can forget everything else and focus on your float.

PAYING OUR DUES

In the early days, Dad and I fished at a pull-off near Penticton. The season started there first. We huddled just north of the prime fishing hole, with short, hand-me-down rods, watching enviously as Joe, fishing like a machine, filled his five-gallon bucket with fish. The limit in those days was 25.

"How many do you think he's got in there?" muttered Dad. "50?"

"More like 75," I said.

Joe was not one to be troubled with "limits."

"Perhaps he is fishing *our* limits," I joked, bitterly.

Dad didn't laugh. We had a few fish each, perhaps a half a dozen between us, nowhere near a limit.

But then we were recreational fishermen. We were there to get away from our problems and to have some fun. For Joe, fishing was deadly serious. It was about survival. Even though he no longer *needed* fish to survive, Joe still fished as if his life and the lives of his children depended on it, as they once had. We hadn't reached that point yet.

The other men who fished with us at the pull-off in those days wore modern snowmobile suits, which kept the wind out. We wore old clothes that didn't. We were freezing.

The men were gentlemen, though. They did not comment on our lack of suitable clothing. They just allowed the natural consequences of our choices to teach us to dress in layers and to seek out clothing that would keep us warm and dry. One good wave could soak cotton pants. When the cold invaded, it came like conquering soldiers. You were chilled to the marrow and the exciting adventure of fishing became torture.

Eventually, I learned that a shell to break the wind was an asset. We both learned that proper head gear was crucial, and Dad bought a snowmobile suit with a hood lined with faux fur. I was jealous.

That suit hangs in my closet now. I wear it when I go snowshoeing or when I'm working outside. The upper left pocket is torn – probably snagged on a branch on one of our walks in to the Rock – and it no longer contains Dad's handkerchief. The suit is no longer waterproof. These days it keeps me warm until it gets soaked by wet snow. Then it chills me.

Back in the days when we were learning how to fish, Joe clenched his pipe between his teeth, while he worked his float masterfully against the howling wind. He could put the float, without tangling his line(!), on any square inch within the arc of his reach. The line attached to the rod was about 12 to 18 inches longer than the pole. The float, depending on where you were fishing, was about three feet from the hook. That meant you had a potential arc of water in front of you slightly less than twice the length of your rod. The ribbon of dark water passed through your arc.

It was not often that Joe missed a bite, but when he did he lifted the float and moved it back 18 inches so the hook would once again pass over the interested party. This master's technique, not yet in our repertoire, often resulted in a fish.

We hadn't yet realized that fishing for white fish is unlike anything else in the world, so we fished only in our arc, waited too long in dead water, or pulled too early at the end of the arc. The dance of the float was still a mystery to us, and we wasted too much of our attention on stamping our feet, wriggling our toes in our boots, thinking about the cold, and shuffling to keep warm.

You're not supposed to worry about your body when fishing for white fish. You're supposed to get outside of it. You're supposed to float.

Joe taught us that. He cast, watched as his float danced along the water in front of him, and just before he started fishing dead water, lifted out a white fish. After a quick check of his hook, perhaps the addition of another maggot, he cast back into the wind. Each deliberate movement was spare and efficient. There was no wasted motion, energy, or action. He had no time to see what we were doing, or that we sat like hunched ravens in cold weather, our ragged clothing fluffed out like feathers trying unsuccessfully to trap our body heat.

We hadn't yet learned that casting into the wind meant holding the hook in one hand while moving the rod with the other hand, and letting the hook go at the precise time for it to land perfectly on target. It was a choreographed dance. Instead, we let the wind push us around, tangle our leader around the float, or twist the main line into a bird's nest. Joe just ignored us.

We got the message. It is impossible to catch fish while you untangle your gear on the shore. Fingers numb from the cold are clumsy, and delay and lengthen the process.

We learned that the rules of fishing are unspoken. We learned them the hard way, by breaking them and suffering the consequences. We learned that each person was entitled to his space, a 180-degree semicircle that fanned out in front of him. If you violated the space of the person beside you, they would let you know. It didn't take too many words or too much deliberate eye contact. Every correction stung like driving pellets of snow.

We also learned that two experienced people can fish fairly close together. The trick is to be in synch with your neighbour. To fish in close proximity, both parties have to have excellent control of their casts and have to be aware of where the other person is in their journey through the arc. It is frowned upon to have your float in the way of your neighbour's next cast, or to make your neighbour wait for you to clear the beginning of his. Your neighbour shouldn't have to shorten their cast because you are their space.

To cross your neighbour's line with yours is the most disrespectful thing of all. We learned this while our fingers were as numb as the white fish lined up in a bag in my mother's freezer. It didn't matter that we did it to each other all the time. Crossing your father's line, or your son's line, is not the same thing. To cross another person's line means that they have to stop fishing and recast. It also means that if they have a bite they will be hampered by your line, and the two lines will probably tangle. If you get tangled with your neighbour, you will be told to move further away from the prime water – *now!*

Such banishment was problem enough back then, but our older, donated equipment, damaged by long, rough use, was shorter than the new equipment of experienced fishermen, and provided less access to good water – and there was little enough of that to begin with. Further from the prime water was a good place to tangle lines in the wind, but a terrible place to catch fish. That was the point.

We got it. We learned a lot on those rocks along the shore, before they straightened the highway. Progress. But they destroyed the prime water forever, that magical place where conditions were perfect. It was where we made our mistakes, paid our dues, and learned from the masters. We *did* try fishing there after the road work was completed, but it wasn't the same. We didn't go back.

Now the pull-off and the prime water is just a pile of rocks that tumbled down from the cliffs above and got pushed around by the highways crew, oblivious to the people driving past – people who didn't and still don't understand the significance of this place, that the mysteries of the universe were solved there, and human relationships became untangled.

THE POINT

The Point we fished from was a jumble of rocks at the base of a cliff. Sometimes we called it the Rock. This outdoor cathedral was where we cast our floats against the wind.

We had to be shown this secret and spiritual spot. We would have never found it on our own. The cliff face was solid behind us and the rocks below, scattered by some unknown architect, formed the platform from which we fished.

My father's rock was much like a bishop's bench in the chancel, the raised platform at the front of a church that holds the altar, the pulpit, and the lectern.

Traditionally, churches are built with the chancel facing east. The narthex, the church entrance, is to the extreme west. The nave, where the congregation sits, looks much like the prow of a ship, which makes every church Noah's ark, moving sinners to salvation. The centre aisle, straight and true, points to the one true path.

Not in our church! Its chancel faced northeast, directly at Squally Point across the lake, and at Ogopogo's pavilion of water-filled caves. My father sat on the bishop's chair directly behind the pulpit – always reserved for the preacher. At the Point, it was a flat, rectangular boulder.

In some churches, the altar is fixed to the wall, and the minister turns his back to the people when praying. If you look at it that way, our congregation was the trees and rocks behind us, and the remnants of the cliff face, which stuck out along the shoreline like a nose.

Our church had an extra feature, too. In its early days, the lake had created a channel through the rocks under our feet. As the waves slammed into it, we heard the hollow clop of water hitting the solid rock at the end of the channel, then the chuckling of the little stones on its raspy breath out. The result was that sometimes a fish that came off the hook before we could grab it and throw it in the pail would find its way back into the lake by falling into this channel.

"Sometimes the rocks eat them," I remarked one day.

We tried to dig the escapees out. Sometimes we were successful. Sometimes. Eventually, I filled in the channel with rocks so that a fish caught was truly *caught*. But I missed the sound of the lake breathing, and the shifting of the little rocks beneath our feet.

I stood at the lectern, from which a layperson could read from the scriptures. At the Point, this rock sloped at an awkward angle. It was difficult to stand there, slightly off balance, feet pointed dangerously downward to cold water. It was even more treacherous when the rock was glazed with ice.

The baptismal font at the Point was the size and shape of a basketball and was positioned much nearer the wave line. The wind and the height of the waves determined whether I could stand there or not. It was no problem on a calm day, but when waves welled up a foot or more of water washed over the rock with each crest.

A flat rock behind us, where I cleaned fish, was the altar. This was where I placed my rucksack, which held extra hooks, line, floats, and knives.

We worshipped at this Point. We clung to the rocks like awkward camels, desert creatures with the wrong kind of feet for slippery rocks. We went there to be connected to each other, in communion with the whole congregation. We pondered the big questions, and the little ones, all looking in the same direction, out at the water, to focus on our float. We listened to the wind and the waves join their voices to create solemn hymns. We did it for three short weeks every year.

Much like a traditional church calendar, a white fish year is divided into sections. Unlike the church calendar, which was full from Advent through Christmas, Pentecost, Easter, Assumption and on and on, the white fish calendar only has only three parts: preparation for going white fishing, actual time on the Rock fishing, and reminiscing and reliving events that occurred on previous trips.

As soon as we stepped from the car on our way to the Point, we assessed the potential of our trip. Could we hear the roar of the waves crash in the semi-darkness? Was it cloudy, or could we see stars shining down at us? Was there snow on the ground, which would make the lectern treacherous? Did our walk along the shore take us on crunching leaves, or did we lose our footing on slick and slippery ones?

The worst was when the snow came early. On those mornings, the path was clearly visible, winding through the trees ahead of us, but the rocks were hidden in three or four inches of snow. Soon we weren't walking so much as blundering. It was a long blunder to the Point around the lake. It was a rite of passage.

One's faith and knowledge were always challenged.

RICH UNCLE

Once or twice a year, my aunt and uncle made the trip over the mountains to visit us. Cherry season was a favourite time for them. They both loved cherries and, after eating their fill in a U-Pick orchard, picked some more to take home. Their visit usually included fishing, too.

When I was growing up, I thought my uncle was rich. Every time he saw me, he reached into his pocket and brought out a dollar. A dollar! My aunt and uncle had no children of their own. They did, however, sponsor me with those dollars. Through World Vision, they sponsored children all over the world as well. They did it for years – even longer than it takes to raise a biological child.

They lived in a house in Calgary that had a magic cupboard. You placed empty glass milk bottles in one side of the cupboard, and the next time you opened it there were full bottles of milk awaiting you. We were astonished. We had never seen anything like it.

Before the cherry years, we lived in northern Alberta. Though we had no cows of our own, we got fresh cow's milk every day from the neighbours, who ran a dairy. One of my jobs was to walk over in the evening and bring back the milk for the next day. The trek wound through bush, across a field, past grandmother's house, past the barn, to the milk room. Our milk was waiting there for the return trip home. There was no charge for skim milk – which was fed to the pigs and provided to us free. We only paid for whole milk.

I hated this chore, so instead of doing it right after supper, while it was still light, I usually put it off until it was dark. By then, the bush was a little frightening. As a result, I always begged one of my sisters, Kathy or Rose, to go with me. Often, I would pull pranks on them along the way. I'd get them to stand under a snow-laden tree, then I'd kick it and run before the snow came down and covered me. My sisters would be covered in snow – at least until they grew accustomed to my tricks or refused to come with me.

Uncle George worked hard and brought in good money. He drove a flashy car – a cherry-red high-end 1966 two-door Pontiac Parisienne – not a practical one like my father. George loved that car. He was the kind of man who kept a shammy of real animal skin in the driver's door, ready to clean off any bugs or dirt from a drive.

He was also the kind of man who mowed his lawn in one direction, and then all over again at a 90-degree angle to the first cut. I never understood this, although going over the same grass twice did ensure a very even cut, and the hash marks left by the lawn mower wheels made a pleasing pattern.

I loved my uncle's visits in the cherry years, but fishing with him was tedious. I had to bait his hook, watch his line, tell him when to reel and when to lift his rod. It was exhausting. And not only was he totally hopeless at fishing, he didn't know when to stop talking. I had to listen to his nonstop jabbering about everything and nothing. Mostly nothing. It was almost more trouble than it was worth to take him out to the Point and help him to keep his balance on the slippery rocks, while baiting his hook, taking off his fish, and watching his float *and* my own. One icy day, I was unable to keep him from falling. The rocks left huge bruises on his legs that lasted for weeks.

To be clear, I am not against talking while fishing. Sometimes talking is necessary. Sometimes talking is a way to give and receive information. At other times, talking is intrusive and silence is a welcome respite. I had one fishing partner who talked incessantly about losing his job at the mill, and about being shafted out of 30 percent of his pension. Admittedly, it was a sad story and the situation had affected him greatly, but after you have heard the same story three or four times on the same day, you pray for silence.

My uncle died last year. He was 94. He is not the only person who once fished with me who has made his last trip to the Rock. Our fishing teacher, Ephram, is gone, too, as are the men he fished with. Ephram is the one who generously took us to the Rock and shared its mysteries with us. My father is also gone; he no longer sits on his stone bench commenting on the wave action, or that the fishing is good, or that one of his church members is near death.

What I have now are memories – for instance, a magical moment when the family gathered after my father died. I had taken a tree branch that had been carved by beetles, and had sanded it and applied layers of varnish. (My plan was to make "talking sticks," imitations of an ancient Indigenous tradition, in bulk and get rich.) Real magic, though, happened when we began to pass the stick around the room. When each person held the stick in turn, they shared something about my father. I was spellbound. As inept and clumsy as Uncle George was in the boat or on the rocks, his big fingers lacking the dexterity to deal with the wriggling maggots, he said deeply meaningful things about my father and about the impact my dad had made on his life.

One of the things I inherited from my father was an accordion. I call it a squeeze box. I remember it sitting at my grandfather's house, behind a chair in his living room. After my grandfather died, it was kept in my father's basement. Now it's in mine. It originally belonged to a woman named Emma. You see, when my uncle got to marrying age, there were no available women who were "suitable," in the community. This is code for German-speaking Christian, precisely in that order. My grandfather, being a practical man, sent to Germany for a suitable bride. Emma arrived, along with her accordion.

Things did not work out. Emma did not like George. She seemed to have a fondness for many of the numerous men in the community, including my father, yet she had a decidedly noticeable dislike for George. There was no magic. There would be no marriage.

George went to my grandfather, who was responsible for Emma's support, and said, "Either she goes, or I go." George was a great help to my grandfather on the farm. The message was clear. My grandfather could not risk losing George. Emma had to go.

My grandfather took her to the city, found her some work, and returned to the farm. Why exactly the accordion did not accompany her to her new life, I don't know. Later, my uncle *did* marry a German woman, who was also a Christian. He loved her for half a century, until death separated them. I still have the accordion.

Uncle George eventually left the farm and worked for Robin Hood Foods. He loaded 100-pound sacks of flour into rail cars, sometimes carrying two at a time on his shoulders. Mostly, he worked the night shift. His work allowed him to buy mispackaged puddings and cake mixes at a discount.

My father, in comparison, was a country preacher. He had a modest salary and four children to feed. We couldn't afford anything as decadent or as luxurious as a pudding or a cake mix. Yet, in Calgary, the man who always had a dollar in his pocket for me every time he saw me, the man who had the magic cupboard, that man, my uncle, had boxes of pudding and cake mixes – boxes of them! – at his disposal. He was generous and more than willing to share. We even got to take some of the bounty home with us.

One time my father went with my uncle to work. My father could not carry two 100-pound sacks of flour on his back, but he could do one. He was not in the same physical condition as my uncle and the next day could barely move. He never tried it again.

My aunt Lena worked, too. She was a seamstress at The Bay. Because she also enjoyed an employee discount, their Christmas tree was bejewelled with the most ornate and breakable Christmas decorations that money and an employee discount could buy. It was a spectacle of wonder and delight.

To this day, I don't know what possessed me to go behind the Christmas tree. I *do* remember the resulting crash and the breaking of the pretty decorations. I remember my father's disgust as the vacuum came out and sucked up the carnage, and the look of disappointment, embarrassment, and anger on his face. I think he looked a lot like me, watching Uncle George fishing. As strange as it sounds, I know now that it is a look of love.

LIFE BETWEEN FISHING, DREAMING ABOUT FISHING, AND CLEANING FISH IN THE BACKYARD

We often went to visit Grandpa Rath on his farm in southern Alberta. Jacob was an accomplished storyteller. My grandparents had fled from Russia, where they'd had fields and orchards. They were hard working and industrious ethnic Germans. The Communists called them *kulaks* (basically, "wealthy peasants") and labelled them oppressors and enemies of the state. Many members of my family were jailed, and their property was seized.

Jacob often dismissed things he did not understand by saying, "That's English." Things that came from the old country, however, were dependable and good.

There was a family myth about something very special brought from the old country. The soil of the family farm near Odessa was lush and fertile, a rich dark loam with very few rocks bigger than your fist. Since my grandparents were good Germans, they made their own sauerkraut. Part of the process involved soaking cabbage heads in brine. To do that, my grandmother placed a stone on top of a round wooden board, which weighed the cabbage down and kept it submerged in the crock, where it could finish the fermentation process.

A rock of this type was a rare and precious commodity in a country without rocks. Not only was it necessary for making sauerkraut, it was vital to the family's survival. According to family legend, when they fled Russia other items of value were left behind in favour of the stone, to ensure that they could make sauerkraut in their new home.

After my grandparents travelled halfway around the world with this heavy and awkward rock, which seemed to be constantly underfoot, they saw the Canadian landscape. They cried. In this country, there was nothing *but* rocks.

This story always came to mind when I was balancing on the icy rocks on the shore of Okanagan Lake in November. It makes you think about how the world is all woven together.

On one visit to the farm when I was quite young, one of Grandpa's cows was calving. Something went wrong and the calf died. The cow was very weak. Grandpa was certain she was going to die too because she just lay on her side and would not get up, although he did what he could for her. I was very concerned about the cow, too, and did not want her to die. I asked if it would help if I brought food and water to her. Grandpa humoured me by agreeing that it might help. I took food and water to the cow for several days, putting it close to her head where she lay.

When we returned home, I put the cow and my concern for her to the back of my mind, distracted no doubt by schoolwork and my regular life. My grandfather, however, remembered my kindness as the cow recovered. He credited me with saving her – though I doubt I had much to do with it. A year or so later, he asked me if I remembered the sick cow and how I took her food and water.

"Yes," I said. My long trips – with a pail of water heavy in one hand and scratchy hay under my arm – to where she lay next to the far fence in the corral came back to me.

"The cow recovered," he said. "I sold her at auction."

Then he took out his old billfold (which I still have), pulled out 11 $20 bills and counted them out in front of me: $220 dollars. It was the most money I had ever seen.

"You saved the cow," Jacob said. "So she belonged to you. That means her sale does, too."

I was overwhelmed that a little kindness on my part had gained such a large reward. Unlike my grandfather, I've never used the billfold. And unlike the heavy rock, I'll never throw it away.

REDEMPTION

When my father was alive, he was only accessible to me through fishing. Now, more than 20 years after his death, it is the same thing.

It's true! I rarely think of him gardening, preaching, playing the guitar, or yodelling, though he loved to do each of those activities. I primarily think of him cleaning a fish or sitting on his perch at the point, catching one.

The last pictures I took of him were in his backyard, after he'd cleaned some fish we'd caught. The pictures were forgotten in a camera and only developed a year after his death. We couldn't believe how tired he looked. Why had we not noticed the signs? Even so, the pictures were a little gift to us – my father, with fish in each hand, standing under the crabapple tree in his backyard in Vernon, a bemused smile on his face.

While we were fishing, Dad and I talked. We didn't do it anywhere else. For example, if I thought my boss was being unfair, I could share that; or if I had concerns about my children, or if money was tight, or if someone was causing me trouble.

There were no phone calls and no interruptions on the Rock – it was just us, the elements, and the fish, beyond the scrutiny of my mother, Crystal, and of my former wife, Laureen, who thought fishing distracted us from completing more important tasks. Fishing for white fish, in particular, seemed to them a huge waste of time.

Our fishing was never about the fish, of course. We carry so much around with us: worries, fears, concerns, dreams, guilt. Guilt is second guessing yourself.

I had guilt. I had left a good, steady job to sell life insurance. Talk about selling the family cow for some magic beans! It was a disastrous decision. Sure, there was potential for success, but for every person who was successful, there were a thousand who had risked it all and were in a worse position than when they began. After that, I had enjoyed working at Canada Post, but I would have had to move to Vancouver and walk around in the rain for five years in order to get back to the Okanagan. I dismissed that option out of hand, but was that the right choice?

Later, I had guilt about my government job. Yes, it was secure, as secure as you could get, but it seemed to cost my soul. The huge machine of which I was a very small cog was clumsy, made baffling decisions, and sometimes spent a million dollars to save a nickel. I was outspoken about the hypocrisy, the lack of consistency, the smoke and mirrors, and the bitter realities I encountered on a daily basis. The ship we were on was being piloted by madmen. At times it seemed we were destined for the rocks.

My opinions were not only discounted, I was told straight out that it was not my job to think. No one wanted to hear it. My job was to shovel coal, not to navigate the ship. I wanted to help people, but the actual people I was helping didn't know of or appreciate my help. The people I dealt with, for the most part, were not helped. I took away their guns, drugs, booze, and charged them penalties.

I also had guilt about my oldest son, Jonathan, about how well I was meeting his special needs, which were putting a strain on my marriage. A friend told me that my efforts to save my son were like a man trying to save a wild fox. The man cares for the wild fox, holds it under his coat to protect it. All the while, the fox is eating his intestines. Was I risking my marriage for my son? Was that the right course of action? Was I living up to my potential? Was I the husband, father, son, and brother, that I had the potential to become?

I often worried about money. When given the choice to earn more money or spend time with my family, I would most often choose the money and work overtime, even if it meant cancelling an important family event. I was worried about my marriage. I was afraid of being alone. That was my greatest fear: dying alone.

Sitting on the Rock and fishing for white fish forces you to clear all of that away and focus on one thing. It wasn't a waste of time; it was needed therapy to help me cope with life.

I sent a note to my youngest son's teacher one time which read, "Please excuse Aaron from school tomorrow. He will be participating in a one-day, highly intensive, hands on, stress management workshop." When Aaron returned to class the next day, the teacher asked him how the workshop had been. Aaron didn't know anything about a workshop.

"You went to a stress management workshop yesterday," the teacher reminded him.

"Naw, we just went fishing," Aaron told the teacher.

My father listened attentively to my concerns. My father loved people, but he was not good at the politics of the church. In his world, love trumped politics. Love trumped everything. Not everyone saw it that way, though. That's why the best times I remember having with him involved fishing. Not church.

I've talked to my youngest sister, Kathy, about this quirk. She said he took her fishing, too.

"I went," Kathy said, "even though I didn't like fishing. I just wanted to be with him."

In my father's view, spiritual depth was about the capacity to love others – to think of them and treat them as he would treat himself. What were their needs and wants? Where did they hurt? How could he help?

The worst times with my father were his absences. He wasn't there to help me with my homework, for example, except at college, when he did my German translations for me. We read the passages together. He tried not to do my work, but it was evident that I was hopeless. He translated. I wrote the words down. If he could have taken the final for me, I would have received a better grade.

I loved it when he was around. Once, before I started school, we were on holidays at my grandparents' farm in southern Alberta. There were no meetings to attend and no services to prepare for. On that holiday, Dad taught me to print my own name. My full name. I was five. He taught me only upper-case letters. My mother had been a teacher. When I proudly showed her the shape of my name, which marched across the paper in a disjointed jumble with a slight slope to the right, she chided my father for teaching me only capitals. I continued to be proud of my accomplishment, until I understood that in her opinion my father had somehow damaged me. This is perhaps why he was not there to help with my homework and decided that fishing was the path to lead me to redemption, both in school and in spiritual matters.

I *do* remember him helping me with a report on religions of the world. I had done the research, and he typed it on his typewriter, the one he had ordered with custom keys so he could type in Portuguese. This wasn't as much fun as fishing. For either of us.

So, we went fishing.

LEPROSY

I was born in Brazil. I remember the tastes of exotic fruits and vegetables, like mango, papaya, and persimmon. My mother made an avocado pudding with milk, lemon juice, and sugar. Whenever I taste that pudding, it takes me back to a time before I had language.

Each day we ate black beans and rice, which were cooked with some tomato paste and onion and a little piece of meat for flavour. Each night my mother carefully sorted the beans and examined each one for a worm hole. Those were discarded. She then put the beans in water to soak. Any beans with worm holes that she had missed would float to the top. These also were discarded.

We did not have running water on demand. We did, however, have indoor plumbing. The city only turned the water on at random times. No problem. My mother left a tap open. When she heard the water come on, she filled every water-holding container she could find – bathtub, pots, pans, and pails. This would be all the water we had until the next time the water came on, sometimes days later.

I had my own bedroom. The walls were sticky because when the house had been painted the workmen had thinned the paint incorrectly. It never did dry right. My room was between the kitchen and the bathroom. You could sit on the toilet in the bathroom and have a direct view of the front door. If you were in the bathroom with the door open and someone dropped by, they could see directly into the most private room of the house.

Next to the bathroom was our maid's room. This was off-limits. Next to that was a storage room (also off-limits) and then the door to my dad's office (even more off-limits). Then came the front door (off-limits), the living room (off of which was my parents' bedroom), and back to the kitchen, with its woodstove.

I did not like kindergarten, which was out the front door. Some kid had bitten me. Each morning I would say that I had a tummy ache to try to get out of going. It worked at first, but when I tried that trick every day my parents soon caught on.

In kindergarten I learned a song: *"Marcha soldado, cabeça de papel."* It means "March soldier, with your head made of paper."

Also out the front door was a very mean dog. He stayed outside to protect the house and yard from intruders. He bit both my sisters and me. I think he even bit my mother. The only one he would listen to was my father. When I came home from kindergarten, I had to stand at the gate and cry out, *"Pai (pie-eh),"* which meant "Dad!".

Dad would open the window in his study and call off the dog. Then I could enter the yard and house.

The church was literally across the street. Beside the church was the parochial school. I didn't go to school there. Behind the school was a park with trees and churrasco pits – Brazilian barbecue – where large chunks of beef or pork were roasted over open fires on metal skewers the size of swords.

We were not allowed to play in the backyard of the house because poisonous snakes lived in part of it, but even back then I was not very obedient. There was also a septic tank, with a rotten wooden lid. I can't image what falling through that would have been like.

On one occasion, I was throwing a knife into the dirt back there. (You never know when having good knife-throwing skills might be important.) The knife was part of a set of child-sized eating utensils: spoon, knife, and fork. My initials were engraved in the handle of each of them. Sadly, the knife hit a rock, which broke part of the blade off. I was busted for being stupid. And for being in the forbidden yard.

Although the backyard was pretty much off-limits, our garage was not. I rode my tricycle or my jeep in there. I also found a knothole through which I could observe what was going on in the neighbour's backyard. Klovis and his family lived next door. Klovis was older than I was, and seemed much taller than me. He was old enough to have the privilege of playing across the street in the park behind the school. Klovis's mother would call him home for supper. She would stand at the edge of the street, and in a loud high-pitched voice would shout "Klovis, *venha para casa*," which meant, "Klovis, come to the house." Then she would stamp her foot, getting her elbow involved to add extra emphasis. The sidewalk and entrance to our garage was on the side of the fence away from the mean dog. I thought it would be a good game to also call Klovis home, including the stamping of the foot with some elbow English for good measure. Klovis's mother was not impressed that I mimicked her actions and she spoke with my father.

Klovis's mother had interesting parties in her backyard, seemingly without fear of snakes.

My father was too busy to pay much attention to me; he had eight parishes. Some of those parishes he started by holding services in people's homes. My mother and I had to go along.

I don't remember the services. I *do* remember that one of these houses was built on stilts, with floorboards spaced so that dirt could be swept between them to the mud below. The woman of the house explained this to my mother, who was simultaneously scandalized and envious of such an arrangement.

I liked it, too. While my father held his service upstairs, I was in the mud beneath the house, looking up at the cracks in the floor, chasing the geese and causing a ruckus to the chagrin of the faithful upstairs, who were trying to concentrate on the message.

During our early years in Canada, my father had only five parishes: three churches; his family, and fishing. Typically, a parish congregation was a collection of God's people: young, old, rich, poor, devout, and lukewarm. Most were farmers. A few had jobs in town or were teachers. There were widows and babies, and children to fill a Sunday school, with kids my own age.

Three churches meant three services each Sunday, and countless, endless meetings. My father was gone every night, which was not very good for his fourth parish.

When we moved to Kelowna, my father had only three parishes, the church with services in two languages mind you, his family, and the Point where we fished.

At the third parish, the Point, my father passed on to me important lessons: how to be a man, how to work, and how to control my emotions. This was a delicate business. Just like his boss, my father was a fisher of men. In my case, he was a fisher of boys. I had to be brought into the fold, nourished, and taught the Word – and to stop chasing geese.

Being a member of three parishes – the church, our family, and the Point – was confusing. Before I understood the mysteries of the sacrament, for example, I was often tasked with disposing of consecrated wine left over in the chalice. It simply could not be poured back into the bottle.

"Pour it in the snow," my father said, "but cover it up. And don't let anyone else see what you are doing."

I did as I was told, but I wondered what it all meant. It seemed wrong, but my father would never ask me to do something wrong. I was in a quandary. My classmates, the sons of farmers, did not have the experience of disposing of consecrated wine, and then covering it with snow, or having to ponder about the meaning of such an act. I envied them.

Eventually, I became rebellious. That was my solution. I challenged my father and tested his boundaries and his patience. I came home from church, still in my Sunday clothes, and test-fired rockets from my nuclear arsenal, directly at him.

"I don't believe in God," I declared.

My mother was nuked, demolished – her world annihilated. Not even the cockroaches had survived the attack. My father was cool. He caught the nuclear devices in mid-air, bit off the warheads, and crunched them between his teeth like they were more delicious than my mother's cooking. That sent me back to my workshop to construct better nuclear weapons.

In my defence, I hadn't wanted to hurt him. I'd just wanted to see what he was made of, to see if his faith was unshakable.

I also hadn't intended to hurt him years later, when I shook his hand on my way out of church one morning. I'd been reading about shaking hands and the message given by a firm grip. I had taken the message to heart. To show Dad that I was a man, and his equal, I looked him in the eye and shook his hand with a firm grip. It wasn't bone-crunching, but he cried out in pain and turned away, trying to free his hand from mine.

I felt ashamed. I hadn't wanted to hurt him. I was just practicing a firm handshake! I was deeply embarrassed.

This was before we learned that the leprosy my father had contracted and that had been dormant for years was reawakening and eating away at the nerves in his hands.

He had probably contracted this painful disease from giving communion to a woman in Brazil. Parts of her face had been eaten away, and her mouth, covered with a cloth, was a gaping hole. He moved the cloth aside to administer the bread and wine. He took his finger and pushed the host in. If he was afraid, it never showed.

He was given medication to treat the condition. His symptoms improved. Years later, his doctor told him to stop taking the medication because all the symptoms had gone away.

Unfortunately, without the medication, the leprosy bacilli returned, eating his nerves and causing him agony. It was first misdiagnosed as scleroderma – a hardening and tightening of the skin. My father had red blotches all over his body. He went to the hot springs in Banff before he knew he had leprosy, with his patchwork of red patches in full display, and commented that he should hang a sign around his neck that read "leper."

Sadly, it was true. Yet despite the misdiagnoses and bad advice, he forgave the doctor. He described his hands as being on fire and often placed them on the cool glass of the car window as he drove.

I would have sued the doctor for that error. My father didn't even consider it.

"The doctor did his best," he said.

I scoffed.

"He was unfamiliar with leprosy," my father said. "He made an honest mistake."

I would not have been so understanding, or forgiving, but then I am not the man my father was. He tried to teach me that forgiveness was more powerful than revenge and that love always trumps hate and anger. It is a lesson I have struggled with all my life.

Eventually, my father had no feeling below his knees. On one of those numb days during those numb years, my parents were in a rush to drive down the valley to Penticton, where my brother-in-law, Cecil, was opening his own shoe store – his lifelong dream. My father busied himself with loading the car. As he backed out of the driveway, the car wheel drove over something in the driveway, but he was in a rush, so he drove on.

When they arrived in Penticton, my parents walked into the shoe store with flowers. It was then that Cecil, the shoe specialist, noticed that my father was missing a shoe.

I noticed it, too, because I was back on his driveway in Vernon, staring at it.

Once again, I told my father to sue. Once again, he refused.

At his third parish, the Point, my father taught me that if your lure is below the fish, you are too deep and won't get a bite. And if you are fishing too deep in relatively shallow water, you will also snag bottom.

"Okanagan Lake is a very deep lake," he taught me. "It is unlikely that you will hit bottom, unless you are on the edges of the lake, which is where you catch white fish."

Sometimes people are deepened. I think that leprosy deepened my father. He had some pretty deep places, dredged through pain. From experiencing the fire in his hands as his nerves screamed out in agony about being attacked by the disease, he gained a capacity to love people and to relate to those who were dying or in pain. People loved him for this. He related to them like no one else could because he lived it.

Though for a time he walked and talked among us, even the pain hadn't made him part of this world. He was an innocent. Once, he went to register a boat trailer that he had purchased from a member of the parish and discovered that the man had never registered it. My father was told he needed to get the signature of the previous owner – who was dead. His widow was in Italy. My father was stymied. How could he obtain the signature of a man who was dead?

Cecil and I knew instantly what to do. We walked out to the street with the transfer papers in hand and five minutes later walked back in with the required signature.

Some might say my father was naive, but I'd say he hadn't let the world harden him. At times, it even looked to me as if he was ill-prepared to survive, quickly reaching into his wallet and giving freely, even though his salary was modest. He let God speak through him.

I would probably be happier today if I had paid more attention to Jesus' words and my father's example about generosity and forgiveness. Jesus was pretty clear about forgiveness. He spoke about it from the cross. My father lived it. I was more like Peter in the garden, who drew his sword to cut off the ear of the high priest's servant when they came to arrest Jesus. I wanted to do battle with evil and to protect the good – even with violence if necessary.

When I think of myself holding on to things, I think of the joke about an elephant who comes to a river for a drink. As he approaches the edge of the water, he sees a snapping turtle sunning himself on a log in the middle of the river. In a rage, the elephant charges into the current, pulls back one of his huge front feet, and kicks the sleeping turtle so hard it flies across the river and is stuck in the mud of the far bank. A nearby crocodile observed the whole thing and asked the elephant why he had done that. The elephant replied that 25 years earlier, the same turtle had snapped at his trunk at this very spot as he had come to take a drink.

"What an incredible memory you have," the crocodile said.

"Yes," replied the elephant. "Turtle recall."

Perhaps my father knew of my difficulty with forgiveness. "If you want to beat a dog," he often said, mysteriously, "you will find a stick." He also said, "A man convinced against his will is of the same opinion still." Perhaps that is why he demonstrated forgiveness over and over, to change my will. It is a lesson I know in my mind but still need to learn in my heart. My anger and fascination with revenge rolled right off him and left only compassion.

Not everything was a lesson. In 1980, the year I graduated from university, my parents returned to Brazil for a visit. They asked me what I wanted them to bring me from there. "A knothole," I answered. They found this to be an unusual request, but when I explained to them that I remembered spying on the neighbour through a knothole in the garage, they understood. They told this to Dr. Craidy, who delivered me. Dr. Craidy went to his workshop, found a piece of wood with a knothole in it, sanded it down, added the coat of arms of Ijui, and placed a picture of Ijui behind the knothole so that once again I could look through the knothole and see the city of my birth. He also added a couple of hooks and turned the project into a key holder.

I still hang my keys on it today. They open things.

THE TWO OSCARS

Two members in the second of my father's first Canadian parishes were both named Oscar. Both were German. Both liked to fish. They treated my father with reverence and deference.

In those days I had not yet reached my rebellious phase, where I wanted to test my father and see what he was made of. The two Oscars often took my father fishing. As I got older, I was taken along, planted between my father and an Oscar in the front seat of the pickup, forced to move my legs as the gears were shifted, not quite understanding the shifting pattern or how to anticipate where to put my legs so I didn't get in the way. I knew the shifting coincided with the engine roaring but could not tell if the stick would move up or down, left or right. The shifting seemed random. My legs were always in the wrong place.

Now my knees are wrecked. I think perhaps in part because they were in the way of the gear shift, and partly from my practice of running up and down stairs two at a time. My own truck is an automatic and has cruise control, so I can move my legs and stretch the ruined one so it is not too stiff when I climb down.

Both Oscars had a boat and a trailer to tow it to Kelly Lake, which is in the territory of the Kelly Lake Cree Nation. The lake was past the church in Goodfare, Alberta, where my father served his vicarage. Both Oscars are probably buried there.

I drove out there a few years ago. It seemed such a long way when I was a boy, but when I flew down the road on this trip I drove right past the church the first time. I only recognized it after I was well past it and had to go some distance further before I could turn around.

I slowed down on the way back, to actually make the turn into the parking lot. The gravel road I knew as a boy had been paved, but the church was the same, with the cemetery alongside and stretching to the west. The old log parsonage was all but falling down. An addition made to the church before my father's time had not blended in well and made the church look uncared-for and haphazard.

In Kelly Lake, we mostly caught northern pike, which we called "jackfish." Jackfish are sleek and snake-like. They have the head of a crocodile, and an equal number of impressive needle-sharp teeth. They even have teeth on their gill rakers. You have to be very careful with jackfish.

I remember fondly the smell of wet burlap, which held our catch on the bumpy ride home. I sat between the two men. I was often exhausted, so as they talked in the glow of the dash lights as we jostled and bounced along the gravel road, I often succumbed to sleep before we reached home.

One time, we were out with the younger of the Oscars. Dad was casting with a large, heavy spoon, which sprouted a sharp treble hook. On his back swing, he hooked the baseball cap from Oscar's head, then cast it out into the lake. Quickly realizing what he had done, he retrieved his line, towing the cap along the top of the water. When it reached the boat, Oscar reached down, freed the hat from the barbed treble hook, squeezed the water out of it, and placed it back on his head. Fishing continued with another cast, as if nothing dangerous had happened.

The older Oscar was said to have caught a 40-pound jackfish through the ice. To successfully bring a fish that size through an ice-fishing hole is a remarkable feat. He garnered much respect for that accomplishment. It is more than 50 years since I heard of that success, and I am still in awe.

THE FISHING TEACHER

My brother, Dan, and I were fishing at the Point.

"We'll catch dinner, Mom," we had said earlier.

What we'd really meant was, "We don't know how to talk to each other except in the language of fish." That's what we were really doing at the Point. We were practicing to read and speak float language.

Ephram was our fishing teacher. He was as old as his name, which came from the tribes of Israel that fled Egypt. We would have been lost without him, just as the Israelites would have wandered aimlessly in the desert without Moses.

Taking two boys to the Point was a lifelong commitment. You can't take back a secret, just as you can't un-ring a bell, or not eat forbidden fruit after swallowing it.

Ephram not only introduced us to the Point, he gave us bamboo poles. You can't buy poles like that. Not anymore. To have poles like that you had to have bought them years ago from a store in Edmonton that is no longer in business: single shafts of bamboo, cut into lengths, the longest segment about five feet long. The segments were joined by metal tips, either by screwing together, or with male and female ends held together by friction. The top segment tapered to a narrow tip barely the diameter of a flimsy twig.

I named my rod "Spindly," because he was 14 and a half feet long and at his thickest point not much bigger in diameter than my middle finger. My father's rod was an amalgam of fishing rod and wooden dowel (perhaps a broom handle), secured with a nut and bolt. It sat at an awkward angle, like an A-frame house, so we called it "A-frame," which also sounds a bit like Ephram, who had gifted it to him.

Ephram was a serious man of few words. In the car, he only spoke directly to my father. In German. When he entered the car on our fishing trips, Ephram greeted us with a curt nod of acknowledgement or a "Hello," at most.

Ephram attended the German service at First Lutheran Church in Kelowna, which was held at the same time as Sunday school, which meant I never saw him at church – unless my father needed me to serve as a pall bearer. Then I joined the grim-faced men. Ephram and I each took a corner of the coffin.

In the beginning, Ephram carried us at the Point, too. We were little more than dead weight, unskilled and undisciplined, lacking focus, daydreaming, and making jokes between each other. We missed more fish than we caught. Ephram always gave us a share, which reflected his generosity more than our effort.

Gradually, though, we learned how to focus on the float. Eventually, we caught more fish than we missed.

One morning, Dan and I got to the Rock early. Two hours later, at 10 a.m., Ephram emerged from the trees on the trail. He was pushing 90 and was winded from the long walk in. I didn't imagine that we would soon be carrying him. He was sturdy and practical and seemed invincible.

He was certainly old school – a big man who lived in a tidy house with a huge garden one street east of ours. He was kind, and of few words. He smoked his own homemade cigarettes – not many, but from time to time I smelled the rich tobacco smoke as the wind carried it towards me.

Ephram came from a tradition that respected a preacher as the spiritual leader of a congregation, the person who fed the souls of the people and who guided them on the path to salvation. That's why he gave my father the best place on the Rock. I think he realized that my father needed to be there and that his sons needed to see him there.

That morning, Dan and I had wanted to shorten the way to the Point, so we had taken a shorter route, down the steep mountain sides that separated us from the highway above. It worked great going in. The scramble down the steep slopes to the lake cut our walk time in half.

Climbing up the mountain with our gear and a bucket of fish afterwards, though, was so exhausting we never did it again. The muscles in our legs ached, and our backs were knotted in pain. In the end, we were no faster than Ephram, who just plodded on.

But I'm getting ahead of myself. At 10 a.m. when Ephram first came out of the trees, he said, "Hello. How's fishing?" For him, that was a whole paragraph.

Before my mouth could form words to answer, Dan hooked a fish and yanked it hard from the hidden world beneath the thin membrane of the surface of the water and into our world of mountains, trees, air, and our fishing teacher.

Dan is not a specialist in finesse. He is more flash than substance. He wants the attention a clown receives and will do almost anything for a laugh. He *really* jerked that line.

The fish swam through the air in a perfect arc like the sun swimming across the sky in time lapse. Just before the arc should have encountered the horizon, the fish hit Ephram on the cheek, and flapped on the rocks trying to get back into the other world.

Our teacher wiped the slime from his face and trundled 50 feet further away from us. Perhaps he sensed that despite our lack of skill we would somehow learn, and that his investment in us would pay dividends for years after his death.

We did learn. And we remembered his widow with a bucket of fish nearly every time we went fishing. Perhaps she thought of Ephram when she ate them. Perhaps the taste of those fish reminded her of their years together, and of his quiet manner and low-key sense of humour. She seemed grateful for the uncleaned fish, and for the embrace of former times. Somehow, he had managed to pass through the veil, and even after he was dead managed to provide fish for his wife – a little bit of himself, invested in us, paying interest.

The longest conversation I had with Ephram was a confession of sorts. It took years to earn enough of his trust to bear the weight of this story. Ephram, the quiet, solid citizen, had once poached a Canada goose, one of a flock that frequented the parks in Kelowna, making a nuisance of themselves year-round, eating the grass and soiling it. For Ephram, who had retired to Kelowna because of its warmer winters, the geese were a reminder of feasts on the prairies. He looked at those geese with hunger and longing. His desire became a plan, which he executed with precision. He fashioned a hook out of wire, which he snaked through the grass, grabbed a surprised goose by the foot, and dragged it backwards to his van, which was waiting with the door open.

It was like setting a hook, I could see that, then battling the flailing bird as he dragged it backwards to the getaway vehicle. Once inside and the door closed, the goose was bonked, the wire stowed, and the getaway made.

He never did it again. "The goose tasted muddy," he said, "not like the grain-fed geese on the prairies."

People are like icebergs. We see only a little portion and know nothing of the rest. We never really knew our fishing teacher at all.

The white fish, though, tasted like Eden at first light, mixed with a steady wind from the south. I never asked Ephram's wife what they tasted like to her, and, yes, I'm still carrying him, proudly, on my shoulders.

THE BEST PLACE TO FISH FOR WHITE FISH

I never learned to fly fish. I do have a book. And a fly rod. I even have a nice selection of flies. I am, quite honestly, in awe of fly fishermen, their light gear and their precision. Fly fishermen can place a fly on any piece of water within reach. They pump out the stomachs of their first fish to examine what it had been feeding on, find a pattern in their tackle box that resembles it, and catch more.

Catching mountain white fish is beautiful, too. It is all about being in the right place at the right time. These white fish, smaller relatives of lake white fish, will be at the Point on November 15. November 11 is too early. It is understandable that you will want to try on the 11th, but the reality is that the fish won't be there, not in any numbers. You may catch one or two, but not the 50 you could catch on the right day. You will tell yourself that next year you will wait, but realistically you won't. November 11th is a day off and you will try anyway, even though you know in your bones it is too early.

I always felt a little squeamish about Remembrance Day. My grandfather was German yet fought in the First World War for the Russians. Because he was German, they stationed him in Turkey, and because he could read and write, they put him in charge of loading and unloading ships. This kind of family history is a good reason to avoid the Remembrance Day ceremonies and to push the white fish season by going early instead, even though it is a dress rehearsal for the real performance.

The white fish come to spawn and stay for a maximum of three weeks. You can fish to the end of the first week of December, and that is all. You may try to drag out the season but, realistically, for the two or three fish you will catch it is better to wait a year.

When you factor in the days you have to work, 21 potential days will soon boil down to six days, maximum. Six days out of a whole year is not a lot of time to be out on the Rock. If you can work magic and change your shifts to afternoons, you can fish the morning and still make it to work on time, but that will only buy you a couple more days, at best.

The right place is also important. Okanagan Lake is 80 miles long. It stretches from Vernon in the north to Penticton in the south. There are many places where you can catch white fish along its shores, but there is only one point where they come like a promise: a rock across Okanagan Lake from Squally Point.

Legend holds that deep under that point is the lair of a lake monster called Ogopogo. I'm convinced that Ogopogo is there, because I've been under the water with my float, staring over at his seat. I even thought I saw him above the water on two occasions.

The first time, I was in a canoe at night with two of my school friends. One of them was housesitting a place on Okanagan Lake, behind the hospital. The house was huge. It came with a swimming pool *and* a canoe.

Housesitting being what it is, we eventually found ourselves on the lake, down by the bridge. We paddled up Mill Creek, as far as we could anyway, then back to the lake. Then I saw something shiny and liquid reflecting the lights from behind me. It had the slimy scales of Ogopogo!

Not quite. As we got closer, a Canada goose grunted and swam off, annoyed at being disturbed.

The second time I thought I saw Ogopogo I was looking down over the lake from a pullout on the highway above the Point. There was a dark line in the water. It moved with the waves. As it undulated across the lake, I was mesmerized. It *was* the famed lake monster. It *had* to be. Then the line became a flock of ducks that took flight and flew away.

My father only spoke of the Ogopogo in a joking manner. He accepted the cartoon version of the Ogopogo, the one used to sell ice cream, and its goofy statue at the foot of Bernard Avenue. But nothing other than that cartoon version of Ogopogo had a place in his world. If he caught a large fish, or snagged bottom, he always smiled and suggested with mock alarm, "It was probably the Ogopogo." He didn't believe.

Not all Christians felt that way. Years ago, a Creationist came to Kelowna. He believed in the existence of the Ogopogo and wanted to find evidence so that he could use it to disprove the theory of evolution. His argument was that the Ogopogo had not evolved. According to his thinking, this non-evolution placed Darwin and his theory on very shaky ground.

Somehow, this anti-evolutionist connected with my father. Dad was intrigued, especially about the idea of disproving the false religion of evolution, that nonsense that was taught as fact to his children in school. He had already made objections to this instruction. These objections came too late for me, the oldest, but Kathy and Rose were granted time away from the classroom for the lessons on evolution. They spent the hour in the school library instead. Nice.

My father was cunning. He knew I loved the Ogopogo, so although his interest was whetted by the Creationist, he sent me in his place, to escort the disprover to the various places on Okanagan Lake where sightings had been reported.

We started at the cement statue of Ogopogo at the foot of Bernard Avenue, and drove up Knox Mountain to gaze north towards Okanagan Landing. We drove out Lakeshore Drive and spent time at each of the various beaches, scanning the water for any sign of the monster.

Our expedition eventually brought us to the Point. We saw nothing that would prove Creation and no actual evidence of Ogopogo. My heart did flutter, though, for this was the time I saw the line of ducks crossing the lake. We squinted, then peered through the binoculars. It was a menacingly dark, undulating, unexplainable sight we were witnessing, until, as I said, it became apparent they were ducks, and we drove off.

I bet the white fish know the secret of the Ogopogo. They are certainly from the same neighbourhood. They share the same realm beneath the waves. They come to the rocks along the lake to spawn, and we come there to catch them and to contemplate. It should be the same with the Ogopogo, I think.

More than once I found myself staring across the lake and wondering if I might see a sign of the monster. I never did. Worse, spending that much time away from my float resulted in many missed bites. I focused, and re-focused, until there was only the float, and no Ogopogo at all.

Except, I guess, in the hidden realm under the water. I can almost feel him there.

VILLAIN

If you were setting out to create "White Fish: The Video Game," you would need a villain. When West Edmonton Mall first opened, it had a tank filled with sharks. The theme song from the movie *Jaws*, with its *bah-dum, bah-dum, bah-dum* played ominously on speakers beneath the tank. Because of *Jaws*, sharks were the ultimate villain at the time. You need an awesome villain for your video game, too, but not a shark. Sharks do not frequent fresh water.

The wind is not your villain, either. Yes, the wind is bitingly cold. It takes your breath away by forcing itself into your lungs. You panic and turn your head away, so you can breathe. The wind also threatens to push you off balance from your perch and throw you into the water. But it is not the villain. It is necessary, just as the waves are. The waves move the float in a perfect arc. They might also threaten to sweep you into the icy lake, but without them you will have little success.

The better the wave action, the more fish you catch. We came to this appreciation on a day when there were no waves at all. Standing on the edge of slack water, water with no energy, we began to pray for a puff of wind and a predictable steady swell. As wet and cold as we were in the wind, we learned that we needed it, like it or not.

The villain is also not the cold. After all, it is November in the Okanagan. It is going to be cold. Ice will form around the rim of your fish pail. The exposed skin on your face will scorch with wind burn. When you take your gloves off to grab a maggot and thread it onto your hook, be quick about it. Try to expose unprotected skin as little as possible to the elements. The cold doesn't ruin your fishing trip, though. The white fish are triggered to spawn by it.

There is, however, a handy villain *beneath* the waves. A villain must be repulsive, and this one is vile and hard to look at. A villain must be reviled, selfish, and serve its own needs. A villain must bring with it some inherent potential of loss. This villain has that, too. He is a sucker – a bottom feeder.

Suckers are ugly and gross. Their huge scales can be seen from outside the atmosphere. There are no scales on their ugly naked heads. Their small accusatory eyes are wrong, too. Perhaps it is the lack of eyebrows or any structure around the eye. It is just the eye, floating like a roque planet in the middle of the head.

As for the head, it resembles an elephant, devoid of ears and trunk. The lips are huge and puffy. That's to put it nicely. They are healed scars. They protrude from the mouth and act like a vacuum, sucking food from the bottom. Imagine the shame.

What's more, suckers have about as much energy as clots of slimy algae. They are docile swimmers, going through their business at their own leisurely – some would say lazy –pace. They are slimy and strong smelling. The gentlemen who go fishing for sleek white fish call them "coarse" fish. It's a euphemism.

Suckers can easily grow to four pounds or more. That is way too big for your ancient bamboo rod to handle. If you hook a sucker and try to lift it from the water without care, you could quickly break your rod. My rod, Spindly, had nightmares about hooking into a sucker that would break him in half. Spindly quivered at the thought. Trying to lift a sucker out of the water with the same motion as catching a white fish is like trying to pick up a bowling ball with a twig. This action cannot end well.

Because of the great danger suckers pose, you need to remain alert. A sucker will take your whole cork float under the water. That is your first indication of trouble. You need to immediately lay your rod down, though not in a place where it could get stepped on by an onlooker or someone who feels you need help. Set it down with forethought, but very quickly, because you need to grab hold of your main line and haul your sucker hand over hand out of its beloved bottom muck, before deftly sliding it up onto the rocks. The villain will be as surprised as you are.

In "White Fish: The Video Game," success is keeping your float, line, and rod intact. The teardrop hook may be bent beyond repair, but that is a small price to pay compared to the potential of damaging your rod. You can spin electronic dice to see if the hook is bent. You'll pay a forfeit, but it beats starting the level again.

One time my father wasn't paying attention. He lifted too vigorously on a bite. It wasn't a sleek white fish attached to his hook, but a loathsome sucker. The rod broke from the strain. The top third floated on the surface of the water, towed by the troubling sucker. Dad had no alternative but to wade in after his rod. He went into the lake up to his chest and retrieved the broken tip, sucker still attached. He did not have chest waders on. Did he stop fishing? Of course not. Don't be silly.

Suckers come for the white fish eggs. They are opportunists. They vacuum up white fish eggs by the thousands. They may also vacuum up your maggot-covered teardrop hook. That is when the trouble begins. Suckers don't want your hook. You do. You just don't want suckers.

I could not imagine eating a sucker, though my grandfather did. When they first came to Canada, the family was so poor he went down to the local slough and caught suckers, not to fertilize the garden, like I did, but for the dinner table. His techniques and theories about catching suckers went with him to his grave, although, really, when you are fishing to live, your technique is different than when you are fishing for fun. I guess.

My dad never suggested that we eat a sucker. We were poor, but never *that* poor. I imagined the meat would be strong, unpleasant, and muddy tasting. I didn't want to find out. He knew, I think. He probably ate suckers more than he wanted to as a boy.

I used to throw suckers back. Then I decided that was not very smart. Why should I give that sucker another chance to break my rod, and more opportunity to gobble up white fish eggs? Just to be nice to all creatures? Come on, this is a villain. We love to revile villains.

After that, I killed any that I caught, and laid them on the shore for the birds. I didn't do this for long, though. Their ugly eyes, distended lips, and look of dismay and accusation was more than I could bear.

Later, I took them home and buried them in the garden, not complaining about the taste of the tomatoes that grew in the enriched soil, or about the extra weight in the pail on the walk out.

My father got very excited when he had a fish on, sucker or not. One time he hooked a jackfish and was standing up in the boat while he reeled it in. As the fish neared the boat, he said to me, "Paul, get the net." I told him that he was standing on it, but he did not hear me. Again, he told me to get the net. Again, I told him that he was standing on it. The fish was nearly at the boat when he told me a third time to get the net, and for the third time I told him that he was standing on it.

Giving up on me, he tried to land the fish without the net. He had the fish out of the water, and nearly in the boat, but it was too big and heavy. As he lifted it, the fish smacked into the top of the gunnel and broke free.

The fish was lost. My father turned to me with fire in his eye.

"Paul, I told you three times to get the net," he said.

"And I told you three times you were standing on it," I answered.

We laughed about that incident for years.

Now *I* am the one standing on the net. I focus on the wrong things and don't hear the instructions. While I'm driving I stare too long at what I think might be a bear or a moose, and my wife, Lisa, cries out in alarm, because we are headed for the ditch. The other day, I looked out and saw an extra black bucket beside the three stumps which stand to the east of my garden. I was trying to think what planter that was when I realized it was a bear. He was eating the dandelions. He should have been fishing. It was too late in the year to try to gain weight with greens. I should have been fishing alongside him, too, but was trying to batten down the hatches for winter. The forecast said it might snow the next week, which was wrong, because there was still so much to do.

We ate any jackfish we caught, although to me it seemed like too much work to separate the meat from the sharp bones. My mother always cautioned us about swallowing the bones. Apparently, when she got her first period, she had been unprepared by her mother. When she started to bleed, she was convinced that she had swallowed a fish bone and was bleeding internally and was probably going to die.

"They will," she said, "pierce your innards and cause internal bleeding."

Part of the problem was that my father was not very good at filleting fish. Like me, he considered filleting to be very wasteful, so we picked the meat from the sharp bones, being very careful not to swallow any. We always had a piece of bread handy, to help remove any bone that caught in our throat. To us, a piece of bread was like an emergency firehose, or an antidote to poison.

Once, Dad caught an even bonier fish, a sucker. When the villain was almost to the boat, he told me that he had a fish on and to net it. He didn't know it was a villain yet.

The first thing I noted was the size of the fish. Compared to the sleek torpedoes we had been catching, this was enormous – more than five pounds. I netted the fish and instantly understood why my father had struggled. We had strayed into shallow waters, and he had picked up a sucker from the bottom. This was not supposed to happen to either of us. To make matters worse, the sucker had inhaled the hook, which was now firmly lodged deep within its throat.

Dad had a hold of the villain by the lips, trying to free the hook with his pliers. The fish moved, as did the pliers, and then my father's pliers were holding the fish securely by the lips. I laughed so hard I nearly fell off my seat. Eventually he retrieved the hook, the sucker was dispatched for his date with my tomatoes, and fishing continued, but in deeper water.

Dad and I often contemplated the meaning of suckers in the world, just as we contemplated all things out on the lakeshore. We discussed them for hours, mostly in silence, with a word or two now and then to catch the wave crests of the conversation. The result, though, was always the same; we were simply unable to see their value.

The Bible teaches that Jesus, when he returns, will separate the sheep from the goats. The sheep will go on the right and the goats on the left. The sheep will be invited to inherit the kingdom prepared for them.

As we contemplated fishing, and being caught, my father and I juggled the mysteries of faith. Deep within us, though, was the fear that perhaps we were the coarse fish, the goats, the ones destined for the garden, and not the desirable ones, the sheep.

Well, Dad has left this conversation, but I'm still having it in the lake that has become where I live most deeply. I know in my head that I am precious, that God loves me. In my heart, though, if I am honest, I secretly fear that I might be the ugly sucker, the undesirable, the reviled, the villain in the video game of my life.

I stand on the rocks, gasping for breath.

FISHING COSTUMES

Because of the cultural significance and importance fishing for white fish came to have in our family, we named the three special weeks of the year when the white fish came to the shores of Okanagan Lake to spawn, the "White Fish Festival." We treated it as if it were Christmas and Easter, in fact the entire church year, rolled into one. This was more to counteract the negative forces of those who criticized the size of the fish, how coarse they were, and who claimed that fishing for them was a waste of time. In response, we elevated these three weeks to festival status. Who could criticize that? There were no parades, but after Dan moved to the coast we were always excited when he returned home to fish with us like the old days.

My costume for the White Fish Festival was a mélange of layers of clothing, gathered over the years from various places. I started with a set of scratchy long johns. I added a turtleneck sweater to prevent the wind from forcing its way down my neck to trouble my back. For pants, I often wore jeans or track pants. Over these I wore a pair of my grandfather's overalls, and on top of all this a wool sweater, and over that a heavy coat. Like the overalls, I had inherited the coat from my grandfather. It was very warm but weighed at least 12 pounds. Depending on how cold it was, on my head I wore either a baseball cap or a brown toque that I had inherited from my sister Kathy. On my hands, I wore a set of hand-knit wool mittens, which fit into a set of leather mittens. On my feet, I wore a pair of felt pack boots.

My father just wore his green canvas snowmobile suit and felt pack boots.

We were not concerned with how we looked while we were out on the Rock. We just wanted to be warm, to protect ourselves from the ravages of the November weather. We laughed about what we called the traditional White Fish Festival costume – like it was the traditional dress of some obscure, remote tribe.

In contrast, for work my father generally wore a suit. On Sundays, of course, he removed his jacket and wore a cassock (which we called a gown) over this shirt and tie. In later years, he wore a white surplus over the black cassock, and stoles which he changed in relation to the church calendar. I like to think he learned something about layering from me.

When fishing was over, we took off our fishing costume and put it in the laundry pile. These garments could be soiled by fish slime, fish milt, the insides of maggots, and they smelled like it.

After church, while my father shook hands, then took off his vestments, turned off the lights and locked the door, Dan and I stole away to play Ms. Pac-Man at a local pizza joint. Ms. Pac-Man gobbled up our quarters almost as fast as we gobbled up the little dots on the screen to avoid the ghosts that chased us. We always intended just a couple of quick games, fully aware that our mother would soon have Sunday dinner on the table. Sunday dinner was the high festival of the week, the pinnacle of family life. We did not want to be late – for dinner, or for my father's quiz about the sermon.

All of this was later in my father's ministry, after he had started to wear a clerical collar. I don't know why. Perhaps it was to demonstrate to us that he was our spiritual leader as well as our father. Perhaps he wore it because his friends and peers wore one. He certainly did not seek attention or recognition. He was much more low-key. He often introduced himself as Ernie Rath – not even his actual name, but a nickname.

The clerical collar consisted of two parts. The first was a shirt with a special collar that accepted the second piece – a flexible white strip of plastic – and held it in place. In the magical time between church and dinner, while Ms. Pac-Man gobbled our quarters, my father would relax and remove that piece of irritating plastic. Sometimes when he took it off, he showed us drops of sweat that had formed against it.

"I seem to be hot under the collar," he joked.

We stared.

I think now that for Dad removing the collar was a sign that he could relax, that his work was done – at least for a while. Sometimes, though, if he had a meeting later that day or in the evening, he would tuck the plastic collar into his pocket until it was time to get hot under the collar again.

After Dad died, Kathy and I dealt with the funeral home. They asked us to provide clothing. We decided to bury him in one of his suits, wearing the clerical collar.

Something bothered me about this decision. I couldn't put my finger on it exactly. I knew my father was dead. I knew he would not go with me to the Rock again. But I also knew that whenever his work was done he took off that bit of hard plastic that dug into his jowls, much like I discarded my tie when my work day was done. I didn't want him to have that piece of plastic bothering him. I asked the funeral director to take off my father's collar after the visitation, just before the coffin was closed, and to place it in his pocket. His work in this life was finished.

I still think about that collar. Perhaps he had worn it to let his parishioners and the community know that he was a man of the cloth. Perhaps he wore it to remind me of the same thing. It seemed out of character. He was usually relaxed and unassuming. When he was young, he was so shy that he hid behind the stove when company came over. He had to overcome that shyness to be able to stand in front of people and share his faith, or to play the guitar and yodel. I did not think he needed to have that piece of plastic as he approached the Pearly Gates. I figured he would do fine on his own.

To be honest, I asked for his collar to be removed more for me than for him. In the complex relationship of father and son, pastor and parishioner, I found it easier to think of him having finished his work and relaxing, without having to wear the vestments of his station. He was more about love than status. Even now, he is teaching me that.

I don't wear ties anymore. Or turtlenecks.

LEARNER'S LICENCE

When you favour fishing at first light, as I do, you have to leave the warm comfort of your bed at 4 a.m., drive an hour, walk along a path littered with rocks, and fend off branches that rake your cheeks and threaten to gouge out your eyes in the gloom just to be rigged and ready when the fish are hungry from the long dark night. There's just nothing like being there at the right time.

In all our trips to the Point, it was more often than not my felt pack boots that took the lead, kicking rocks off the path, breaking branches that tried to impede our progress or that raked alarmingly across our faces far too close to our eyes. I always felt a sense of urgency, a sort of panic or pressure to get there, to get rigged and be ready for the best fishing of the day.

My talented wife, Lisa, who amazes me by the amount she accomplishes and the number of tasks she completes, tells me that I lack this sense of urgency in most other areas of my life. She says that my complacency is illustrated in my mantra, "If it doesn't get done today, there is always tomorrow, or the day after, or the day after that." She says a mantra like that robs me of the joy of completing tasks.

She is right, of course. I have selective urgency. To defend myself, I tell her I love deadlines. I live for the whooshing noise they make as they go by.

Of course, there *isn't* always tomorrow – or the day after that. Sometimes when you put off doing what needs to be done and it gets down to the crunch, life sends you a curve ball – or a truck full of explosives that flips on its side 14 miles up the road with the driver trapped in the cab. All of which actually happened. Your priorities change then, and the precious time you had allotted for digging your gladiola corms before the ground freezes solid evaporates as you scramble to gather warm blankets, a crowbar, and the big hammer. Out here on the Haines

Highway in the triangle that makes up the northwest corner of British Columbia, the closest emergency response is at minimum an hour and a half away. I tell people we do not live in the middle of nowhere, but we can see it from here. Out in this remote area we have to look after each other – there is no one else. The gladiolas will have to wait.

But first you have to learn that even though we are in God's hands, there is no cavalry other than us. We have to look after each other. And when someone is in trouble or needs help, it is necessary that our priorities change.

Before I was able to drive on my own, I had to rely on my father for an early-morning ride. My father was not partial to first light. He took time as it came. He was unconcerned if a service ran a few minutes long, or even more than a few minutes. I heard him say more than once about worship, "Church starts when we begin, and it is over when we are finished."

For example, my father did not feel, as Kurt Vonnegut apparently did, that people come to church to daydream about God. For my father, church was an opportunity to worship and praise, as well as to learn and grow. His relationship with time and worship was unique. It was not a one-hour-a-week obligation or chore. It was a celebration. Sometimes just as the service was winding down and some of the members of the congregation were getting a little antsy, wanting to get on with their Sunday afternoons, my father would ask the choir to sing the anthem again, particularly if it was beautiful or one of his favourites. The choir director was pleased, the choir surprised, but the members of the congregation who were on the one-hour-a-week program glanced at their watches as the choir rose to sing the anthem again. It was not his signature move, but certainly within his repertoire.

At his funeral, the choir anthem was "King of Kings," one of my father's favourites. When we were planning his funeral, one of us said that just before the recessional, we should rise, just as our father would have done and ask the choir to sing the anthem again. At the appropriate time, I was given a nod from one of the pastors, who was in on it too. I rose, turned and addressed the choir director. "If my father was here," I said with a quavering voice, "he would have asked to hear that beautiful anthem again. Could you sing it again?" And they did.

My father felt the same about fishing as he did about any other religious experience. The trick to fishing with my father was to keep warm and busy until he was ready to go home, which was late, because you hadn't arrived at first light. I wanted the freedom to arrive and depart from the Point on my own schedule.

For many boys, the rite of passage to manhood consisted of obtaining a driver's licence. It was the same for me: the freedom to go from one place to another, of being separate and distinct from my parents, and to go fishing at the proper time. The latter was my special addition, but it was a serious need.

The flames of desire to get my driver's licence were fanned into a wildfire when I bought my first car, six months before my 16th birthday. My father and his friend Joe arranged the sale at the Point.

"It's a dependable car," said Joe, between puffs of smoke from his pipe, as he fished like a machine. "It is an insult that the junkyard will only give me $50 for it."

"$50!" I gasped.

The two men turned and noticed me. My father nodded and Joe offered it to me.

Of course, my father wanted to give him $200, but Joe wouldn't hear of it. He would only accept the $50 that the junkyard would have given him.

This beauty was a faded green 1964 Pontiac Laurentian three-door sedan. It was a three-door because the rear door on the driver's side displayed the scar of an accident and wouldn't open. It was beautiful, and it spelled freedom.

The first thing I did was to install an 8-track tape player, with the help of a friend. The player had four channels. By pushing the selector button, the tape would move to one of the four channels and play the song there. I once recorded the song "Lucky Man" by Emerson, Lake and Palmer on an 8-track, so that no matter which track I pushed, I always had that song playing.

That's how I spent the first months of car ownership: pressing buttons. I dealt with the agony of time passing until my 16th birthday in early November, when I could apply for a driver's licence. My birthday is conveniently located next to the White Fish Festival. Time passed as slowly as when dawn brings a clear sky and the shy fish do not come into the shallows. Most Canadians measure time and distance in the rising and setting of the sun, or the time it takes to travel from one place to another. White fishermen measure it in the time it takes between bites, the time it takes when one school of fish passes by your hook until the next one passes by – vast stretches of time. Back in the day, this 15-year-old boy measured it by driving a three-door sedan back and forth in the driveway, and by the number of times I had listened to "Tap Root Manuscript," by Neil Diamond, on the new tape deck. These stretches of time are even more vast.

So it came to be that while I was learning to read my float during white fish season, I was also studying for my learner's licence at night at the kitchen table, and silently critiquing my father's driving habits. In the afternoon, I practiced parallel parking on the street in front of my house, where wooden apple boxes were set up to mark the edges of imaginary cars I was trying to park between. The apple boxes were quite forgiving.

Sometimes, when I grew bored of parallel parking, I drove my uninsured car without a driver's licence, around the block and back before my mother was aware that I had even backed out of the driveway. Always, I studied the driver's manual and prepared myself for the written test.

One summer day, I decided to drive out to Rutland to see a girl I liked. She lived about ten miles away and I thought that if I took all the back roads I would minimize the risk of being detected. My plan worked perfectly, and I was sitting smugly in the driveway of the girl I wanted to impress when her mother called out and told her there was a phone call for me.

My mother had noticed that the car was missing, had figured out my destination, and had called to give me thunder.

"Why would you take such a foolish risk," she asked, "one that you could pay for, for the rest of your life?"

"Uh ..." I said.

"Get home right now!" she commanded.

"Okay," I said.

"We will talk to your father about this," she snapped.

My knees shook and my heart was in my dry throat all the way back into town. I walked right into the house and gave my mother the keys, because I knew my car privileges would be going away for a long time.

Dad woke me one morning; he only ever called me once for fishing. "Paul," he said softly, "put your feet on the ground. We are leaving in 15 minutes."

I smelled coffee on his breath. The aroma of toast and butter clung to him like a cloak. He did not call a second time. I nudged Dan awake. We dressed in our layers and stumbled upstairs for a hurried breakfast.

Soon, we settled into the drive. With all our layers, it was too warm in the car. My long johns were scratchy beneath my shirt. My parka was tossed in the back. Sweating, I peered at the road ahead of us, my excitement mounting as I deciphered the highway signs and the painted lines, which reflected light back from the blackness of the pavement.

Passing wasn't an issue. At that early morning hour, we had the world to ourselves. The only other souls we encountered were workers at Gorman's mill finishing their graveyard shift. The scent of pine filled our car as we passed by.

Sometimes the highway was icy and treacherous. My father crept along, concentrating deeply. If there were other fishermen, they did not know of our secret spot and had spots of their own to get to.

At the lectern, Dan and I balanced on the rocks, clumsy and awkward, our boots slipping on the slick stone. We were two separate creatures, joined at the hip, constantly grabbing on to each other in panic to catch our balance, although it was our fight to keep our own balance by grabbing the other that would cause us to teeter and upset the equilibrium.

Before long, as I stood shoulder to shoulder with Dan, I lifted my rod, then cocked my arm to cast out my hook and float. The hook sailed through the air on the back swing and came to rest under Dan's nose. Time stopped. We took a breath in and out while the hook rested there, my arm drawn back, tensed, and ready to release. The hook did not pierce the skin. It just sat there, poised, the orange of the teardrop bright against the fear in his eyes.

Had I followed through on my cast, I would have hooked Dan by the nose and caused him to lose his balance and follow the hook into the lake, which would have dragged me with him. Instead, he cried out in a panic, and I stopped just in time.

Casting a sharp hook around eyes, ears, and noses is like driving a car. You need to be alert and precise. When driving, you need to stay on your side of the road. When casting, you need to keep your hook and float in your area. You have to be aware of what others are doing. You have to be aware of everything going on around you – in front, to your right and left, and even behind you. A second of inattention can be disastrous.

Although I prefer fishing at dawn, there are some who profess that dusk is as good as dawn. It is true that as the shadows lengthen, fish come closer to shore and are less afraid of the shallows.

The downside of fishing at dusk is that everything becomes harder in the approaching darkness: gathering your gear; not leaving anything behind; stumbling against rocks; walking back along the trail with a bucket of fish heavy as an anchor, lengthening your arm and causing your muscles to ache. There is also the issue of bears, which, like white fish, also tend to be more active at dusk. A bear should be denned up in November, but you never know. Perception is reality. A bush that appears to be a bear is as terrifying as a bear – at least for an instant. Fishing at dusk is a like writing a blank cheque to a person you do not totally trust.

My father drove home slowly. The black ice was back.

As my 16th birthday approached, I began studying diligently for my written driver's licence test. The guys at work teased me by saying the government was seriously thinking of pushing the driving age to 18. I was panicked until I found out it was just a joke.

I panicked because we had moved from northern Alberta to Kelowna just prior to my 15th birthday. In Alberta at the time, you could get your learner's licence on your 15th birthday. I had already missed one opportunity when I was on the cusp of achieving my freedom and had done 13 months of hard time waiting for my 16th birthday. The thought of having the opportunity snatched away from me again was almost more than I could bear.

I went to write the test as soon as I was able. I remember a couple of the questions. One was about driving over a fire hose. The other was about backing through an intersection. It offered several options for making this maneuver. One involved honking, another signalling, and so on. The correct answer was, "You are attempting a highly dangerous and illegal operation." I have always remembered that advice when attempting to back into an intersection, but not while going to visit girls, strangely enough.

I soon had my coveted learner's licence in hand. I drove a little with Dad but spent more time on the road with our neighbour Mr. Kroening. I used to cut his grass with his fancy self-propelled lawn mower. Much later, after I was a seasoned driver, I drove to Summerland and did some serious parking with his granddaughter, but that is another story. Her name was Susan. She told me one time that you have to kiss a lot of frogs in order to find your prince. I was not happy about being a frog. I hope she found her prince.

I had my learners for the obligatory three months, then got a real driver's licence. Freedom. Soon after, I got my first speeding ticket. As I was a new driver, and it was a school zone, I received a letter from the superintendent of motor vehicles advising me to take a safe driving course, which I never did. I was leaving the high school and accelerated to the normal speed limit while still in the school zone.

There have been speeding tickets since. One while we were on a family vacation; the officer also wrote out a ticket for each of the boys, who wanted a ticket too.

A LESSON ABOUT MANNERS

There is an etiquette to fishing for white fish. These are not the official regulations imposed by a government body – published for your convenience in booklet form and distributed liberally – concerning limits, bait restrictions, and so forth, and enforced by conservation officers who can issue fines, seize fishing equipment, and even vehicles.

But, to succeed you need to know the rules. My father told me about a man who caught 40 fish on Wood Lake – in one day. The limit was two. We struggled in the cold to catch two. I was incensed. This was not only against the regulations, it was the behaviour of a boor, a greedy and uncouth person who cared nothing for anyone but himself. Justice was served when the conservation officer issued a penalty of $50 per fish. A $2,000 fine seemed not only justified but just.

The unspoken rules of fishing etiquette are serious. They are the critical lubrication that keeps the machinery of human interaction running smoothly, avoiding friction and irreparable damage. It's like finding yourself in a bar on Cape Breton Island. If you strike a key on a battered piano to see if it is in tune, you *owe* a song to those who heard you strike the key. It must be played immediately. This becomes even more critical if a party was held in the bar the night before and the cook and servers are nursing hangovers. The debt must be paid to maintain the natural order of things.

Fishing etiquette is enforced and adhered to by sportsmen. For example, if a fellow fisherman asks what lure you are using, you are obligated to tell him. You are not obligated to give him one of yours, or to sell him one, even if you have extra, but etiquette dictates you must give an accurate answer. If you soak your hooks or bait in fish attractant, you do not need to disclose this fact if the question was about the lure itself.

The first rule of fishing etiquette is that the first person to the fishing area gets their choice of spots and enough space to fish in comfort until they are finished. No exceptions. No crowding. Some people – certainly not gentlemen or sportsmen, communists perhaps, people who have not spent time learning fishing etiquette – are so brazen with selfish ideas that they are convinced that the entire the lake belongs to everyone, all the time, and that there is no reward for arriving early, or getting out of bed even earlier. Such people will elbow their way into your space, as if it were their right. These souls believe that everyone is equal, the one who stayed too long in bed, and the one who left it early. These uncouth persons demand equality, although proper etiquette dictates that if you are second to a spot you relinquish by your tardiness any and all rights to that spot until the first comer clearly departs. If you are not first to a spot, you're not there at all.

I only violated fishing etiquette twice. Once, I sat on an ice-fishing stool and broke it. The fabric was brittle in the cold and tore from the metal frame. I was embarrassed and fell onto the ice. I offered to replace it, but never did. Not keeping my word was a direct contravention of fishing etiquette. If you break something, replace it. *If* you borrow something, return it in the same condition it was in when you received it.

The second time I breached the rules, I wormed my way onto the Point when someone else controlled it. Dad, Dan, and I had arrived early, but not early enough. We were racing to the Point so we could be rigged and ready, land the first fish, and give the traditional white fish yodel before any others had finished setting up.

Not this time. When we arrived, two strangers were already on the Rock, fishing in our secret spot. One was in my spot, the other in Dad's. I did the polite thing, what fishing etiquette required, and moved 50 feet south of the Point, to set up there. It was not impossible to catch fish at the secondary spot, but it was more difficult. The Point, and more specifically, our spots on the Point, were the magical combination of a million factors all working together to create the perfect fishing environment. Moving as little as two feet in either direction meant compromising on critical factors, such as water depth. The secondary position was a very narrow place, not in the direct path the fish followed. There you could sometimes catch a few fish. It offered barely room for one person, though, which meant the three of us would have to take turns.

I was disappointed and resentful. We had fished the Point ever since Ephram, in his kindness, had led us there through the trees. Taking the secondary position was as frustrating as waiting for a child to dispense his own pop at a soft drink machine. Why a parent would allow a young child to dispense their own pop, trying each flavour, slowing the line, inconveniencing people and preventing anyone else from dispensing their own drink is another question. All you can do is wait and try not to let the frustration mount.

I surveyed the interloper's equipment and technique. Perhaps I could learn from him. My initial disappointment and envy about not getting our spot soon spawned more frustration and then anger. These were not the emotions of a good citizen, sportsman, or Christian. It was like someone had provided tools to a monkey in the hope that it might build a cathedral.

The man in my spot was wasting our precious fishing time by fishing too close to shore. His float was at most a foot from the rock he was standing on. He needed his float to be at least ten feet away from the rocks, on the line where the dark water started. On top of that, his float, which should have skimmed across the water with the elegance and ease of an Olympic ice skater, was not rigged correctly and danced around like a drunken moth. A float should lie flat on the water, scribing a perfect arc in its journey with the wind from ten o'clock to two o'clock. The stick that pierces the float can only telegraph the presence of a fish by standing up. If the stick is constantly in motion, you'll never see the difference and will never set the hook.

The interloper was catching nothing and, judging by his obvious inexperience and lack of skill, wasn't likely to do better with time. It looked pretty clear to me that if he wasn't catching fish it was unlikely he would limit out, or tire of catching fish and move on so we could take his place.

I couldn't stand watching the best spot wasted like that! I moved in. I could do nothing else. I set up shop next to him, in the forbidden zone. Immediately, I began to catch fish, one after another, much to his astonishment and disgust. He looked at me with indifference at first. His expression said that I was merely lucky. He glanced over enviously after I continued catching fish. When Dan joined me and also caught fish, the man in my spot grew frustrated and defeated.

I tried to help him by showing him the hook I was using and how my float was rigged. I explained that his dancing float was a handicap instead of a finely tuned instrument. It was as if he did not understand English. He persisted in fishing exactly the way he always had and caught no fish. Eventually he packed up and left.

Dan and I were so busy catching fish, we didn't see him go. My father did. The disappointed man was almost at the trail when my father called out to him and asked if he wanted some fish. He trudged back, shoulders slumped in defeat, and held a bag open as my father poured in all the fish from our pail with a very audible plop, plop, plop. Then they were gone.

My father did not want me to profit in any way from my rudeness. Fish caught in rudeness, he taught me, are stolen fish. They were never yours.

THE GAS STATION POCKET KNIFE

I have a box of folding knives in my desk. One was a gift from my grandfather. Another is a gift from my youngest son, who also carries a knife on a regular basis. I have a Swiss Army knife from a Swiss policeman. Another I found lying on the ground in an alley in Skagway, Alaska. Some are large. Some have thumb-assist knobs. One was given to me by my ex-father-in-law, to pass on to my son or grandson. Another is cluttered with too many blades, and is childish. This is its story.

My family were not campers. We tried camping with borrowed equipment a few times – just often enough to remind us of all the down sides: sleeping on the hard ground, the bugs, the challenge of cooking with a camp stove, the lack of running water and hot showers, waking up cold and stiff or worse, and the relentless damp.

We experimented with a tent, which smelled of oily canvas, sweat, and mildew. It was complicated and hard to set up. We tried a tent trailer, even though my father was against towing things behind him, or backing them up. The most successful trip we took was in a borrowed motorhome, with all the comforts of home away from home and worse gas mileage. We ended up damaging a vent while backing under a tree branch.

In the tent era, we took a camping trip to Banff National Park, with family friends. They had a boy my age, and another a year younger. The three of us formed a little pack.

We noticed the knives on display at one of the stops for gas. We all coveted the shiny blade that folded neatly into the faux bone handle. Our want became an obsession that burned inside us. The knives, of various colours, were displayed in a cardboard fan, high and out of reach of little fingers. Each fit perfectly into a cutout portion of the fan. In a white sunburst in the right corner the price was written by hand: $6.95.

That was a small fortune, considering the source of my income – discarded pop cans I collected from ditches which could only be traded for two cents; and beer bottles, which could be traded for five cents. That meant that the knife of my dreams represented, at best, 139 beer bottles lifted from the mud or rescued from water. Sometimes a mouse had crawled inside a beer bottle and died. The partially rotted corpse had to be shaken out. This was not an easy task. If you could avoid getting splattered, especially in the face, that was a bonus. The mice did not go into clear bottles, just the amber-coloured ones. As an adult, I refused to drink a beer from a bottle for many years because of that experience.

The high asking price for the knives was even worse if you factored in pop bottles and cans, which were worth almost nothing. I wanted the knife badly, though. I did not purchase it at the first stop, then regretted that decision. I would not make that mistake again. A knife like that would be so handy on the camping trip: cutting wiener roasting sticks, cutting rope, making shavings to light fires with. There were a million things I could use a knife for.

I was relieved to see the familiar fan-shaped display at the next gas station. There was one black knife left. I bought it. It was magnificent and felt substantial in my hand. In my pocket, it felt sleek, grown up, sophisticated and dangerous.

It was only a few days later, at a campsite in Banff, that I was washing the knife at the pump. The pump was situated above a wooden grate. The water was cold on my hands, the knife slippery, and it fell from my grasp, momentarily bounced on the wooden grate, then splashed into a pool of muddy water three feet below. I felt like I had been kicked in the stomach. I couldn't believe it. The knife was gone. There was no way to retrieve it. Even if I could remove the grate, the murky water, like a black hole, obscured all its secrets.

I moped around for a day or two while the other two members of my pack used the knives they had bought and had not dropped into the watery abyss of doom. Funds were tight, but I could manage another knife, *if* I gave up other treats like pop and ice cream. The problem was that we were now camping and so not using gas, which meant trips to gas stations were few, and the likelihood of finding another fan-shaped display seemed slim.

Day followed day. The souvenir shops had knives for sale, but not like the one the black hole ate. In desperation, I purchased a knife from a souvenir shop across from the Wax Museum. The knife folded but was not sleek and streamlined. It had two blades, a can piercer and a slotted screwdriver. Disgusting.

Back on the street, I tested the sharpness of the blade. The blade was sharp and sliced deeply into my thumb. I tried to staunch the flow with the paper bag the knife had previously been stored in. It didn't work. The blood flowed.

Now we were a dozen people walking down the sidewalk in downtown Banff, one bleeding from a self-inflicted wound. I slipped into a cafe, grabbed a handful of napkins, and tried to stop the bleeding.

Somehow my father became aware that I was leaving a blood trail. It was the worst possible outcome. While rendering first aid, he asked pointed questions to determine why I was bleeding from a cut on my hand. I told him that I had been testing the sharpness of my new knife. His scowl hurt more than the cut on my thumb. He told me that in his opinion I was not old enough or responsible enough to have a knife. He demanded the knife, examined it, and then slipped it into the pocket of his jacket.

This hurt more than dropping my beloved knife into the drain. This burned. The wife of the family friend was a nurse. Later that day she determined that stitches were not required.

So what? I had lost two knives in less than a week!

I knew better than to broach the subject of the knife for a couple of days. I had to let Dad calm down.

After I put some distance between us and the incident, I did ask. Dad agreed that I could have the knife back when we got home. My heart sank. There would be no knife for the balance of the camping trip. Three weeks was a life sentence.

The rest of the vacation was uneventful. We spent some time on my grandfather's farm, where a knife would have been handy. My thumb healed.

As we headed home, my spirits lightened. The anticipation kept growing inside of me since Dad had said I could have the knife back when we got back home.

Technically, we were home once we drove into the driveway, but I considered the correct timing of the request. I didn't want to receive an extended sentence by seeming too eager.

We drove into the yard. Before unloading the car, my father went out to look at how his garden had fared during his three-week absence. I followed him. As he appraised the work that needed to be done, I gently reminded him that he had said I could have the knife back when we got home. He reached in his pocket and passed it me. Then he asked if I was going to test it on my thumb again. I assured him I would not.

I still have that knife. The blue writing it once had, which read *Banff*, and the accompanying graphic of The Sulphur Mountain Gondola, is all worn off. Compared to the knives I have gathered since, it is nothing special, perhaps even a little plain and unassuming. The main blade is not as sharp as it once was. There is more than a hint of rust on the can piercer, and I don't have confidence in the screwdriver either, but I've kept it.

Sometimes I still test it on my thumb.

THE WOODEN KNIFE

It helps to have a grandfather who was a farmer in Russia. You can help your sister out of a jam. Here's how.

One of my first jobs was doing farm work. I did a number of different jobs for a variety of neighbours. I helped bale hay, for instance, by lifting the formed bales from the baler chute and placing then in the stooker, a metal platform of welded pipes designed so the hay bales (or straw) sat at a 45-degree angle. We stacked the bales in a pyramid of ten bales. When the top bale was in place, a lever was pressed, which lowered the stook to the ground. This allowed the hay to dry before being stored in a barn for the winter.

I also shovelled pig manure for a widower who gave money to my dad when he thought about it. I never knew if it was by the hour or job or any of those details. All I knew was that I had to load a shovel with pig muck and try to get it through a hole about a foot square, five feet off the ground. Not everything made it through the hole. There was a swath of pig excrement from the floor to the hole. What a strange job.

I also got to pick rocks, which are called winter strawberries. Frost moves rocks upwards to plague farmers. It is one of the things that makes the world interesting. A field that has been picked of winter strawberries will have to be done again in a year or two. A rock bigger than your fist damages farm equipment, which makes working the crops difficult. Picking stones means walking behind a tractor that is pulling a stone boat – either a platform on skids or a wagon. Any rock (or root) bigger than your fist has to be picked up and placed on the boat.

It is dry, exhausting, mindless work, and let's just say not my favourite. Some of the fields I picked had been recently cleared of trees and the roots were often stubborn, even after the heavy equipment was long gone. You can guess that they had to be pulled up, too. It was a contest to see whether the Earth would break me or I would break it. (We haven't quite got to sorting this out yet.)

I also got to shingle a shake roof. The old shakes had to be removed with a scoop shovel, any remaining nails removed, and then the new shakes nailed in place. I had a mouth full of shingle nails tasting as metallic as my blue spit. I can still taste them.

I also bagged fescue, which my grandfather grew to sell as grass seed. Fescue was harvested with a combine and then augured into a truck. The crew waited with burlap bags, which they filled from the auger. There were a million grasshoppers – a dizzying array – some crippled, some trying to escape the insane machine that had gobbled them up and just as promptly spat them out into this reality. Even though I wore gloves and long sleeve shirts for protection, I was itchy everywhere.

Another part of my training for saving my sister Rose was to shovel grain inside the granary as the auger discharged it from the truck. The dust was so thick I could barely see. My job was to shovel the grain into the corners of the granary as it poured into the room all around me. This was long before dust masks or dust filters. I coughed up black dust for weeks afterwards. I took to taking a tea towel and tying it around my nose and mouth as a filter.

"I seem to be missing a tea towel," my grandmother said.

"It's in the laundry," I replied.

Another job I had was helping to castrate the pigs. My job was to capture a pig and hold his legs while the farmer worked on him. First came a slap of disinfectant, then a small slit was made in the sack. One testicle was pushed out, the cord cut, then the other. Another slap of disinfectant and the surprised pig was on his way. The testicles were tossed into the crowd of pigs awaiting the procedure themselves. They gobbled up the testicles of their comrades while waiting their turn.

The thing is, I knew about castration, although I had not actually done one myself. My father's most severe suggested punishment – reserved for those who had committed heinous crimes – was that they should be castrated with a wooden knife so they would get slivers.

And that's the point. Rose was tormented at school by one of her classmates, who was as cruel as only human beings can be. My parents tried to support her against her tormentor and advised her to turn the other cheek.

"Turn the other cheek" was the approved method to deal with tormentors. It was biblical.

It also did not always provide immediate results. The torment continued. I decided to have a chat with the boy. I was at least three years older and liked to throw discus and shot put. I drove to the school – my old junior high – and got there between classes.

I approached the tormentor, grabbed him by the shirt, and held him up against the lockers, lifting him up on his tiptoes so he could look me in the eyes. I said I had heard he was giving my sister a rough time. He asked who my sister was. I told him that he *knew* who she was, and that, more importantly, I knew who *he* was. I told him that if he bothered her again, I would castrate him with a wooden knife so he would get slivers. Then I sauntered out, as only a Russian-German farmer hounded by the Bolshevik Revolution could do.

He never bothered her again. Rose said that if he saw her coming down the hall, he would turn and walk off in the other direction. Smart boy. Don't mess with the Russians.

THE MASTER

ADVANCED TECHNIQUES FOR WHITE FISHING

To rise to mastery at catching white fish, you need to cover your hook with maggots. You can be in the right place, at the right time, with the right gear, but if you have no maggots you will not catch fish. Maggots are a critical component of any successful fishing trip. Without maggots, you are fooling yourself and wasting your time.

Some fishermen swear by mealworms. Mealworms are big and awkward. At best, they are a poor second choice – often forced by panic and desperation – just ahead of the plastic hellgrammite, with its alarming number of legs and other appendages.

A plastic hellgrammite, however, with a maggot attached, is certainly a combination that can be used successfully to catch fish. Using live hellgrammites would also be fine, but in November it is too cold to be out flipping rocks to try to catch them. It is also not legal to move hellgrammites from one body of water to another. You can't stock up.

You can certainly stock up on mealworms. And you have to. Mealworms are filled with a yellow pus that leaks out like custard pudding when you stab them with the hook. Either that, or they break into pieces. They are expensive and are far too scarce in their brittle clear plastic containers. Those containers also don't hold up well in cold weather. The plastic cracks easily, and then the containers leak mealworms into your rucksack. This is to be avoided.

As easy as mealworms are to come by, though, they fail because they are just too wide. You have to wrestle them onto the hook. You end up getting custard pus all over your fingers. Fingers that you will later eat your lunch with. Mealworms are *not* the answer.

Maggots are. Immature maggots, the ones that are wire-thin, are too small, though. In cold weather, your fingers react quickly to the cold by becoming thick and clumsy. Baiting your hook efficiently will be impossible if you're struggling with your maggots.

This is why a good fisherman keeps his maggots warm, and why a great fisherman keeps his maggots warm in his mouth, keeping his hook as much as possible in the water, where the fish are, and his hands back in the warmth of his mittens, where they should be.

We weren't great fishermen. We stored our maggots, each of them about the size of a grain of rice, in sawdust in plastic pill bottles. Of those, my father had a steady supply. We kept them in a coat pocket for easy access, or if it was really cold in a layer under that.

Here's my procedure:

1. Open the lid of the pill bottle.
2. With your index finger, select a likely candidate.
3. Gently roll the maggot up the side of the pill bottle.
4. Gently pinch it and lift it between your thumb and index finger.
5. Thread it onto your hook.

Easy, right!

There were times, though, when no matter how careful I was, a pill bottle slipped from my numb fingers and scattered its precious cargo amongst the rocks.

Between fishing trips, we kept the maggots in the back of the beer fridge downstairs. They were in cottage cheese containers with a whole or two punched in the lid to provide air. In the cool confines of the fridge, the maggots settled down to sleep.

Back at room temperature, it didn't take them long to wake up and move around looking for food. Now, here's an interesting thing. A maggot will only eat rotten flesh. This is why they have been used to treat gangrene. They ate the rotten flesh and left the healthy flesh alone. This is something the son of a leper doesn't want to think about too much.

I started raising maggots out of necessity. It was a disaster to go to the fishing store the day before a trip only to find that they were sold out. The maggots came by plane from commercial maggot producers in Edmonton, but sometimes the weather created an inversion layer, which caused a low ceiling of fog that prevented planes from landing in Kelowna. Too many times I had to rely on plastic hellgrammites, because no way was I using mealworms.

I had a procedure for raising maggots, too:

1. Put some fish heads and guts in a pail.
2. Allow flies access to the pail for three days only. (This is important. When harvesting maggots, you want them to be approximately the same size. If you allow flies to continuously lay eggs, when it comes time to harvest the maggots they will vary greatly in size because they are at different stages of development. You don't want to be groping through them.)
3. After three days, pour off any liquid, add clean sand, and cover the bucket with a board.
4. Wait seven days. (This is biblical.)
5. If it is really hot, seven days is too long. In the cooler weather of September, seven days is optimal.

Obviously, God made the world in August, when six days was just right. A fisherman thinks of these things.

There is a smell associated with raising maggots. The stench of rotten fish is overwhelming. When I harvested, I often smoked a cigar, thinking the pungent aroma of burning tobacco would mask the stench of the rotten fish.

I had a procedure for harvesting, too:

1. Go to Dairy Queen and have a banana split.
2. Spoon a small amount of the sand from the nursery bucket into a flat container. A banana split container is ideal.
3. When the maggots move away from the light, pick up the maggots with a plastic spoon and place them in a waiting container

filled with sawdust. Banana split containers came with long plastic spoons.

4. Put out your cigar.

5. Go fishing.

One morning I was harvesting maggots, then went to pick up my oldest son from school. I must have absorbed some of the maggot stench in my clothing because when he saw me he scrunched up his face and said, "Dad, you smell like magnets."

Makes sense. Maggots might stink, but they are fish magnets because they attract the fish. And that, like a banana split, is sweet.

TEN MILLION DOLLARS

In my father's parish, there were two brothers who were millionaires. My father became good friends with the younger of the two. They were not friends who would go fishing together. They were family friends, people you invited over to play cards with, friends who came to family gatherings like baptisms, birthdays, and anniversaries. They were friends who were so close they could sub for you and attend your son's graduation from university while you were on holiday in Brazil. Those kind of friends.

The brothers had started from nothing. They had scraped together what money they had, bought a gas station, then a rundown motel, then a Ma and Pa grocery store, which expanded to an independent grocery store, that eventually grew to do $100 million a year in sales.

The grocery store was a huge success. It employed more than 100 people. Over the years, Dan, Kathy, Rose, and I all worked there.

The younger millionaire tried a number of other ventures. He had some good ideas, but no matter what he tried, most of these started to consume more money than they generated. He did, however, own a wholesale produce company that sold potatoes to a second distributor, that sold them to the grocery store, which sold them to the customers – so, basically, he earned money three times on the same potato. That was smart business.

It's too bad that nothing else worked that way. Some ventures sucked up money like a black hole sucks up light. He kept pouring money in, as if the infusion of a little more capital would surely turn things around.

Of course, the silver mine in Nevada never produced silver, and the horse ranch in Tennessee never produced the champion thoroughbred – but they could have, and the money invested employed lots of people.

More and more money went into these unprofitable ventures. Like a gambler, he always believed the next big success was just around the corner. He continually borrowed money from friends and acquaintances. Based on his success with the grocery store, people saw these ventures as a sound investment.

They weren't. The younger brother once borrowed money from my father. Just one week before he declared bankruptcy, he visited my father again and asked for more. Surely, he must have known that his financial world was in shambles and would soon to collapse. I had a hard time with that.

In the months preceding the bankruptcy, he was even swindled by a con man himself. The con man had promised to invest $100 million in his businesses, giving him the necessary capital to make things right again. It was a lifeline.

I was ice fishing with Dad on Wood Lake one Saturday at that time, when he let it slip that he had a share of the $100 million. He would be getting $10 million, because he had "invested" with the younger brother. He believed it. In fact, he was troubled by it. Dad didn't doubt the money was coming. He believed that it would, the way he believed that Monday follows Sunday. What troubled him was whether he could "handle" the responsibility of such great wealth.

I was astounded. My father was good with his finances. He was steadfast. He was solid. He was a good steward of all the things that God gave him. He never had much, but he was frugal and lucky, and was able to pay off his home, and have a little money in the bank.

He was Jacob's son, after all. He grew up hungry. He knew how to pull nails from wood, straighten them, and use them again. His grandson, my youngest son Aaron, works in construction. If *he* drops a new nail, he doesn't stop to get it. For him, *time* is money. For my father, leaving the nail would have been incomprehensible. In his life, there was no waste, and no haste.

I was troubled and perplexed. I wondered what big money would tempt my father to do. He was not materialistic. He bought things out of necessity rather than for the excitement of buying them. He would go to three stores to find the cheapest price on a $2 package of fuses. His cars were modest and practical. He only bought one brand new car in his whole life: a cream-coloured 1964 Chevrolet Bel Air.

Before he bought that car, the two of us stopped at the lot in Beaverlodge, Alberta. We were on our way to church in Goodfare, or more likely on our way back, and had some time to kill before the evening service.

Somehow the car was unlocked. I sat behind the wheel. The front seat was covered in plastic, and the car had that delicious "new car" smell.

Dad was excited about that car, too. I think he was in the process of making the decision and wanted to imagine what it would be like to own it.

Eventually, he drove that Chevy over 400,000 kilometres, without having any major work done on the motor. He was quite proud of that purchase and the way it ran. Mechanics would listen to the engine in awe. That car ran like a top.

In later years, my father partnered with a pastor who was envious that my father had paid off his mortgage *and* had travelled all over the world. This was a man who bought a brand new car every year.

"Buy fewer cars," Dad told him.

Obviously, my father wouldn't be tempted by cars. Liquor, maybe? My father did not drink whiskey. At times he would accept a rum and Coke, or a margarita, if someone else made it. He didn't know how to mix liquor. He was, however, partial to Apricot brandy although, simply because it was liquor at all, it offended my mother's Methodist heritage.

On occasion, my father drank wine, even the bad wine I produced and labelled NTB – "Not The Best." My father renamed it "Not Too Bad." He did like beer. I watched him and my uncle drink American beers, one after another, in 100-degree heat. It had to be American beer, though, my father explained, just to keep your water levels up.

I never saw him drunk, or even tipsy. Besides, it would be hard to drink ten million dollars, even in American beer, even with global warming. It would be hard to drink a million dollars of anything – even if he bought wine at $1,000 a bottle or cognac at twice that.

My father lived a straight-shooting cowboy lifestyle and urged me not to "spit in the well, because one day I might have to drink the water." This made sense to me. Spitting in the well was similar to poisoning the well. It was a good practice to avoid. As far as life lessons go, it was up there with avoiding burning bridges.

Gambling? My father didn't gamble. Well, other than making bad investments. He and my mother *did* go to Las Vegas once, though what exactly they did there is unclear. He didn't even buy lottery tickets. He taught us that coveting, which was covered in the tenth Commandment, was a no-go. It was wanting something at someone else's expense. By buying a lottery ticket, you hoped everyone else would lose and you would win.

"That's a sin," he said. "If you want something, work for it, save up, and then buy it honestly."

Getting something for free was not on his menu.

"King David saw Bathsheba bathing on the roof," he said. "She must have been a beauty, because he coveted her, even though he already had 900 concubines."

As a teenager, I did the math; David could have slept with a different woman each night and not have had a repeat for almost three years.

"David coveted," my father said. "He wanted something that was not his. So David transferred Bathsheba's husband to the front, where he was killed. Then David could have her." This was obviously bad. This was something we needed to avoid.

Raffle tickets were also forbidden. They too were covered under the "coveting" commandment. It was comical watching my father interact with someone selling raffle tickets. If the cause was worthy, my father wanted to help, but he didn't want to buy the ticket. This bewildered the person hawking the tickets.

Raising money for cancer research, for example, was a worthy cause. My father, however, did not want the car, quad, trip, or any other prize that was offered, but he wanted to help by making a donation. If the tickets were $20 and my father offered $10, the raffle ticket seller didn't know what to do. They could give no receipt. It didn't matter that my father didn't want one. An extra $10 would make the books unbalanced. Often, they would not accept his donation, and he would not buy their ticket, leaving both parties disappointed and frustrated.

The $100 million my father's millionaire friend needed didn't arrive. There was always an excuse. The man who needed to sign the cheque was away on holiday. The bank could not receive such a huge sum without special paperwork. On and on it went, and the younger brother, the borrower and investor, grew more and more desperate. My father never gave up faith in him.

Thinking I was being helpful, I told my father that he did not have to worry about his $10-million burden. There would be no $10 million. My father looked at me incredulously, as if I had told him Christmas would be cancelled for the next ten years.

"The money is not coming, and will not come," I repeated. "In fact, there is no $100 million and never was."

He just stared at me.

That frustrated me further. "If it comes," I said, in the comical and careful words of a pastor's son, "I will eat your shorts, after you have worn them."

Finally, this was something he could respond to, as a farmer's son. "And, if it doesn't come," he replied, smiling, with just a bit of an edge to his voice, "I will eat yours."

As the weeks rolled by, from time to time I asked Dad how things were progressing with the $100 million. There was always a new reason why their money had not yet come.

My father was losing hope and gaining it at the same time. He was hoping that his friend would get the capital he needed, but relieved that he would not have to face the burden of a fortune.

It wasn't until after the younger brother had declared bankruptcy that my father conceded that the money was not coming. I had mercy on him and did not make him eat my shorts. Instead, I presented him ceremonially with some edible underwear, strawberry-flavoured, like a fruit roll-up he could wear.

I did not disclose where I had come by this article of clothing. In his wisdom, he didn't ask.

NEPHEW

Because my sister Kathy has always been the first to open her home for a family function and is the living definition of hospitality – working herself to exhaustion to ensure that everyone is more than satisfied – it was hard to say no when she asked me to take her middle child, her son Thomas, white fishing with us. Cecil, his father, was a good man. He had a mind for business. Giving the boy the experience of fishing was not in his wheelhouse, though.

I tried to dissuade Kathy. I really did. She was expecting to have Thomas back unharmed and in the same condition she gave him to me, without frostbite, without broken bones or scrapes from the sharp rocks. That was impossible.

"It's cold out there," I said. "It's a long walk from the car for little legs." I was getting nowhere. "We leave early," I added with a clench of my jaw.

Kathy ignored my roadblocks. She wanted to provide this experience for her son. A time was arranged.

Kathy had often been the beneficiary of gifted white fish. We were more generous with uncleaned fish, once the realization of the sizeable commitment to cleaning we had made set in. This realization often came while carrying a heavy bucket of fish along the trail, after the fun was over. We tried everything to save ourselves. We changed hands. When the muscles in our shoulders ached and burned from the strain, we took turns. One carried the rods, and the other the bucket of fish. On one fishing trip, my father, my two sons and I kept 98 fish – two fish under our limit. It was only later that we realized the magnitude of our error. It takes hours to clean that many fish. Hours of bending over the picnic table in the backyard; our hands cold, chapped, our backs aching from working on a table that was too low for the work we were doing.

We never made that mistake again. Whenever given the opportunity to empty our pail, we eagerly slid fish into a waiting sink with a plop, plop, plop. I felt a little guilty about leaving Kathy with the cleaning, but she was happy to receive them. I think.

As the years progressed, we got even smarter. While we were still out on the rocks, we decided how many fish we needed *before* we caught them. Six to this widow, six to that. We remembered the widows not just because the Bible told us to. They were, after all, the widows of our fishing teachers. We owed them a great debt.

Once the list was filled, I would begin tossing fish back, especially the smaller ones. Dad would hear the splash as the fish returned to its world.

"What was that?" he asked, already focusing on his float.

"I think it was a wave," I answered.

It was a game we played. We both knew that catching was much more fun than cleaning. It was even more fun than eating.

On the day we took Thomas, fishing started off well. As the morning blossomed, though, the grey skies brightened and the fish retreated to the dark water beyond the reach of our rods. It was a rare sunny day in November. The bite was off.

Dan and I were ready to go but felt guilty that the nephew had not caught more fish. Actually, in our own eagerness to fish, we were uncertain if he had caught a fish at all. What kind of uncles were we? We decided that on the next bite we would hook the fish, if we could, call the nephew over and have him lift it out of the water, while praising him excessively for his fishing prowess. It was a clever plan born of desperation.

The morning progressed, slowly. Moments marched by, and bites were scarce. To make matters worse, Dan and I were chatting and missed a few bites, which only prolonged our stay and increased the pressure we had put on ourselves.

Finally, I hooked a fish. We called Thomas over, gave him the rod and told him to watch the float. With a fish attached, it was sometimes under the water, and sometimes on the top of the water, moving erratically.

"Pull up!" I told the nephew with excited encouragement.

Dan and I both cheered as he landed the fish on the rocks at his feet. Mission accomplished. We could pack up and go home.

Like generations before us, on our return from the hunt we regaled his mother with the story of his prowess. We praised Thomas again and told Kathy how her son was a great fisherman. We were off the hook.

The next year Dan and I found ourselves in the car with our nephew again, going fishing, and as we drove along we relived incidents that had happened on past fishing trips, as we often do, keeping the culture alive. A big part of the White Fish Festival culture was retelling and reliving the tales of trips gone by.

"There was the time my father brought a good-sized fish out of the water," I said. "It was heavy, and his rod was awkward. He tried to maneuver the fish towards the bucket but overshot. It passed by the bucket and over the rocks to the bank. When he tried to compensate for his poor control, and the weight of the fish, he panicked and overshot again."

"He took the fish right back out over the lake," said Dan.

"The whole time, the fish was struggling," I said, "then it dropped free and was gone."

"We teased Dad about that a lot," Dan said. "'That fish got quite a tour. Here are the rocks, here is the pail, here is where you came from. Goodbye.'"

We all laughed. Sometimes that is how fishing was.

Then from the back seat the nephew, wanting to join in the storytelling, teased us right back: "Hey, remember the time you hooked a fish and gave the rod to me and pretended I caught it?"

Sometimes that's how you get caught as a fisherman. My prophecy was right: we hadn't returned the boy in the condition in which we had received him at all.

DISRESPECTING THE ROCK

As I mentioned, my father was a generous man. He wanted others to experience the magic of our secret place. For my part, I did not want to share my father with anyone. Sure, there were some automatic invitations to the Rock: Dan, my sons Jonathan and Aaron, my uncle George. Okay. Dan added an element of hilarity to the event. He was a clown and his antics on the Rock had us laughing. My sons allowed us to catch more fish, as each was entitled to their own limit. My Uncle George loved to fish, and we loved to have him, but he rarely made it over the mountains in November. If we wanted to bring someone from outside of that close group, my father and I touched base about it.

"I'm thinking of bringing so-and-so to the Rock," he would say, floating it by me.

Once, he wanted to bring a member of his church. I knew the man in question and found him to be negative and vexatious. If you said "black," he would say, "Some might say it is black, but it is more a deep charcoal than black." Churches are made up of a wide range of people, and some of them have very different ideas. I knew that this man had caused my father some grief. At one church meeting, he suggested that the benches of the church should be removed so that the congregation would stand and take a more active part in the service. His off-centre grasp of reality and his tendency to let you know exactly how he felt, made him the type of person I usually avoid.

I was apprehensive but said nothing. Life is too short to get mixed up in other people's negativity. But inviting someone to the Rock was a commitment for life. It is not like we owned the site. Nothing stopped a person from coming back on their own. We had no restrictive covenant stating that they could not go to our secret location unless we were with them. Inviting someone to the rock was like ringing a bell that could never be un-rung, an invitation that could not be withdrawn.

As it turned out, I was right to be concerned. The complaining started in the car and continued from there. It was too early. The drive was too long. The walk along the lakeshore was too long. It was too far. He couldn't see where he was going. It was too cold. He was like a yappy little dog.

I longed for him to be quiet. I wanted his words to freeze around his mouth. I would hear nothing but the wind in the trees, small rocks chuckling in the waves, and the sound of a fish doing a mating dance in the gravel as it was landed.

The brisk walk to the Rock was usually one of my favourite segments of the whole experience. There was the crunch of the leaves as we stepped on them, the pungent smell of pine, the trail that disappeared in places only to reappear, urging us onward. The first part of the trail was broad and flat. It skirted some cabins. I imagined the summer people who enjoyed their time there on the water. We were from different worlds, never meeting, using the same place at different times for different purposes.

About halfway, before the trail got really rough, there was a dock, and a house in the trees on the cliff above. Sometimes there was a dog, and we tried not to disturb the people who lived there, as we quietly moved along the lower strip of their property. Eventually the trail petered out altogether and dumped us on the rocks of the beach for the last 100 yards. It was here that we could assess the wave action, and our excited steps quickened, only to be slowed again when our feet slipped on the wet and sometimes icy rocks.

Even when we were fishing, Dad's guest complained.

"These fish are so small, they hardly seem worth it," he said.

"Some are bigger than others," I answered, "and some of the really small males we toss back."

"There is no reel," he complained.

"A reel would just slow you down," I responded, more cheerfully than I was feeling. "No reel is a big part of the fun."

"People tell me the fish are bony and taste like wallpaper paste," he continued.

"I've never actually eaten wallpaper paste," I said, more sarcastically than I should have.

He was exhausting. After a while, I tuned him out. I had come to clear my mind, focus on my float, be with my dad, and have some fun, not to play verbal judo with a boat-sucking whirlpool.

I cannot remember his name. He was a short angry man. His critical words rattled around the Rock and bore into me. It was like the coarse drill the dentist uses, not the high-speed one but the low speed variant that vibrates down to your toes.

"I will never do this again," he said.

"Fine by me," I thought. "Fine by me."

I glanced at Dad a couple of times during the ordeal. I was seeking a look of understanding that we were bearing this burden together. He was focusing on his float. There was no look of understanding. Nothing at all passed between us.

I'm not saying the Rock is magical. But I will say that we were trying to do a good deed, and were being punished.

I don't remember the rest of the trip. The whirlpool likely complained until Dad dropped me off at my place and then headed north with him.

This disrespectful man was right about one thing, though. He never came back. Long before the white fish season rolled around the next November, he was dead.

JACOB

My grandfather Jacob did not come to the Rock. He was not a fisherman. I'm not sure why not. He was strong and could have easily made the walk. He had enough warm clothing. Some of his clothing made the trip to the Rock for many years after his death, so that wasn't it. Perhaps he knew that the Rock was for my father and his sons, and for me and my sons. Maybe he didn't like white fish. I know, it's hard to imagine, but there it is.

Jacob was of the earth. There was no fishing equipment among the things he left behind after his death. Not even crappy fishing gear. He didn't mention any fishing gear to me the day we went through his tool shop when he was a mere 90 and he pointed out the tools he wanted me to have: the grandfather crowbar, five feet long and an inch in diameter, which I gave to Aaron and now wish I had back and need to replace; a collection of ball-peen hammers and other tools from the "old country"; shovels and hoes polished silver from working the earth; and a Hutterite chest with dovetail corners that belonged to my father and that still smells of mothballs.

"Take these after I die," he said. Not before. He still needed them. He was still planting trees for the future.

Jacob knew how things worked. He understood that the right kind of grease applied at the correct time and in the right place can resolve an impasse. In contrast, my father, the young missionary, waited a month in Rio for his goods to clear customs. He checked every day and was told each time to come back, in a few days. He did not even consider that greasing bureaucratic wheels was not only necessary but sometimes the *only* way to move forward, so he always came back empty-handed.

"What are you doing in Rio?" asked the missionary board. "You've been there for a month."

"My stuff hasn't cleared customs," said my father.

"Well, offer them a bribe, Rath," replied the board.

According to Jacob – who told the following story with a smile and a wink – long, long ago there was a fox and a bear who were rivals. Bear had a lovely long tail, longer and nicer than Fox's. Fox had a beautiful tail – the one he has now, but it was just not as wonderful as Bear's.

Bear was proud of his tail. Too proud. It was spectacular tail, magnificent, not the little stumpy one he owns now. He always held it up so everyone could see it.

One day, Fox noticed a fisherman drill a hole in the ice and catch a nice batch of sleek fish.

So Fox devised a plan. When he saw the fisherman was getting ready to leave the frozen lake, he ran as fast as he could down the trail, threw himself along the track in the snow and pretended to be dead. After a while the fisherman came along. He was very happy to see a dead fox lying beside the path. The fur seemed to be in pretty good shape, too. The fisherman picked up the fox and threw it in the back of his wagon beside his freshly caught fish.

When the fisherman wasn't looking, Fox grabbed a fish and tossed it off the wagon. Then he grabbed another and tossed it off, too. He quickly bounded off himself, gathered up the fish, and began to feast.

As Fox was digging into his prize and congratulating himself on his cleverness, Bear came by.

"How is this possible?" asked Bear, when he saw Fox gorging himself. (Bear was licking his lips at the thought of fresh fish.) "How do you have fish in the winter when the lake is frozen over? This is unheard of. Impossible."

"I can't tell you," Fox replied coyly. "You wouldn't be able to do it."

"Tell me," Bear demanded. "I can do anything you can."

"Well, you certainly wouldn't be willing to ..." Fox said, his voice trailing off. "No," he added, "it is quite impossible. You would never risk your magnificent tail." (Fox was enjoying himself.)

Bear looked at the delicious-looking fish. They smelled sooooo good.

"I will do anything," said Bear.

"Okay," said Fox, "but you can't tell anybody. Not a soul."

"I promise," Bear vowed solemnly.

"I catch the fish with my tail," replied Fox.

"What?" exclaimed Bear in an disbelieving tone. "How?"

"I cut a hole in the ice," replied Fox, "then I lower my tail down in the water and when I feel the fish biting on my tail, I pull them out and feast on fresh fish."

"Show me," said Bear. Fox told Bear to meet him the next day about the same time. Fox waited until the fisherman had left the ice, then went with Bear to the fresh hole in the ice.

"Put your tail down in the water," directed Fox. Bear hesitated. He did not want to get his lovely tail wet.

"No fresh fish for you," Fox taunted.

Bear put his beautiful tail into the icy water.

"It's cold," said Bear shivering, as the icy water soaked his tail. "Should I pull it out now?" asked Bear impatiently, after only a second.

"You must wait," replied Fox.

Bear waited, with his beautiful tail down in the water. "I think I can feel them biting on my tail," said Bear. "Should I pull now?"

"You might have one or two small ones on, but if you really want lots, you need to wait. You must have patience," said Fox.

All night, Bear stood at the hole with his beautiful tail in the water. Fox stood beside him encouraging him to stay just a little while longer. When morning dawned, it was nearly time for the fisherman to return to the lake.

Fox told Bear to pull his tail out. Bear pulled as hard as he could, but of course his tail was frozen into the ice.

"Pull harder," encouraged Fox. "You must really have a lot of fish on. That is more than I ever caught. You will feast for days."

Bear pulled and pulled, but try as he might, he could not lift his tail with all the fish he had caught through the ice. In the distance Fox could see the fisherman approaching at the edge of the lake. This was a good time for Fox to slip away, which he did.

As the fisherman approached, Bear panicked, twisting this way and that until his beautiful tail broke off. Bear was free and ran away from the approaching fisherman, leaving his beautiful tail frozen in the ice. That's how he was left with just the stump of a tail that he has now. Of course, Bear never forgave Fox for the trick he played on him.

My grandfather always finished this story with one eyebrow raised, as if he had shared a secret of the universe. Then he would give a little chuckle as if he was laughing at his own joke. We knew he was wise, and also that he was a little crafty and quick with stories that seemed like they could be true. He was able to talk to animals, too – at least, they seemed to understand him. He spoke in low tones to the cow to get her to move over so he could milk her. He talked to the chickens, and the pigs came when he called them to be fed.

Perhaps he was a fox. We would see him flit around the corner of the pig barn, or being swallowed up by the dark, musty mystery of the cow barn, bucket and milking cap in hand.

Jacob's calloused hands were proof that he was practical, that he knew hard physical labour and how to maneuver obstacles that thwarted his forward momentum. He planted wheat and raised cattle, pigs, and chickens. He butchered and cut his own meat, and made sausage. He was a survivor.

It broke his heart that his second son, my father, did not become a farmer. It broke my father's heart when I didn't follow him into the ministry. Now, I thrust my grandfather's pitchfork into the pile of grass and leaves I have collected over the summer to move it into my newly constructed compost bin. I think of my father and grandfather who owned this fork before me. I wonder if it will outlast me and end up with my son, or his son.

Of the three men who have owned this fork, two are dead. My grandfather used it to pitch hay and to muck out his cow barn. My father used it in his garden to move stacks of weeds and to spread grass clippings as mulch between rows of vegetables. He also used it as a rake, to gather prunings from the peach, cherry, and apricot trees in his garden. Now my own gloved hands on the handle reach back through time to them.

The wooden handle has been worn smooth with use and sweat. It looks like a narwhal's tusk attached to five rusty tines. When I lived in Oliver, British Columbia, I used the fork to shake dirt from sod that I had taken up to expand my garden. My grandfather saw grass as a waste of real estate. In his world, only the dark well-turned earth of a garden was a legitimate use of land. A garden produced food. Grass was just for show, an expensive and useless consumer of time and resources. I believe that grass is good for one thing: making compost.

This fork certainly did not come from the old country, not like the good hammer – you know, the one that had seen two new handles and a new head. A good hammer is made with pride, to last, not like new crap made for one use – if you can get *one* use out of it – and then into the garbage with it.

The truth is, my grandfather brought very little from the old country, except my uncle and my grandmother, pregnant with my father. As I pile my compost, I think about them all. I am making compost for my garden and flowers. I love the smell of the grass and the leaves as they break down and turn back into dark earth.

For my grandfather, growing food was life. Like a bear, he knew that if he did not have enough food, he and his family would starve. Survival drove him from before sunrise to after sunset.

He must have known that trouble was brewing before it arrived in the middle of the night, announcing itself with the loud rapping of the butt of a rifle on his door. Yet there was something more than survival that made him bury wheat in his field. If it was just survival, why not have the wheat in the granary or milled into flour? Why did he hide it? How did he know the box had to be ventilated? Was it one of my father's stepbrothers who had heard that a storm was coming? Were there murmurings in the village square that public sentiment was turning against the German immigrants? Someone is always in the know. Why is it usually the unsavoury people who have the inside track? Did my grandfather foresee that he and the men in his village would be deemed Kulaks, their property and possessions taken away, and the lot of them thrown into jail? Many of them never left those jails alive.

I lean against the fork and think about turning the compost next spring, and using some already made to dress my raised beds. I have a link with these men, more than fishing, more than gardening, more than family, and even more than a mistrust of government. We are all men of the earth.

FOUR-POINT MULE BUCK

One morning, my friend and I went to the Point with our sons. As we neared the Point, I became aware of something moving on the trail ahead of us. It was late in the year for bears, which were usually denned up by November, but you never knew.

In the dim light I made out a four-point mule deer that must have been hit by a car on the highway above us. It was crawling forward, dragging its twisted body. Both back legs were broken and its spine was damaged. The deer could not stand, run, or walk. As it couldn't climb the steep hill to the right, it went into the lake to the left, and swam away from us and the shore. I doubted the deer could last very long in the water and was relieved to think that it would be released from further pain by drowning.

It was sad, to say the least. I had hunted mule deer all season but had been unable to find one. A four-point buck would have fed us all winter. Day after day, my friend and I had scoured the hills above Brenda Mines in his trusty but rusty Toyota 4x4. After all the time and money we had invested, we had nothing to show but memories, and a few pictures of wild country. Here it was, though, the day after the season had closed, and a nice four-point had dropped into my lap, wasted.

When fishing was done, we made our way back down the trail to the waiting car. We had just started on the trail proper when we came to a small bay. The deer had not drowned! Instead, it had circled back and was now too weak to even drag itself back to shore. It was in about two and a half feet of water. Only its head and shoulders showed.

I told my friend that, in my opinion, the deer had spinal injuries and broken legs and was going to die a slow and painful death. I went on to say that it was our responsibility to end its suffering. Because he had been injured and was likely in shock and his body riddled with adrenaline, the meat would not be suitable for human consumption. My friend agreed with my assessment of our responsibility.

"Any suggestions?" he asked.

We had only fishing rods, and one knife. We did not have a gun of any kind.

"The deer is tired and weak," I said. "If we get a good-sized log, we can get it onto the deer's head, force it under the water, and drown it."

My son Aaron looked dubious, but we agreed to try. After a scramble, we eventually found a suitable log, lifted it onto the deer's antlers, then forced the deer's head under the water. It was under the water for a long time. Air bubbles rose from its mouth and nostrils. Just when we thought we were done, in one last valiant effort to survive, the deer used his remaining strength to lift his head and drink in the sweet, sweet oxygen that had been denied him.

We were stunned. We had tried to end the suffering of this poor animal, but had just added to it, and had tortured him more.

"Fuck," I said, because sometimes only that word will do. I unsheathed my knife and waded into the cold waters of Okanagan Lake. I stepped carefully on the slippery rocks and moved close enough so I could grab the deer by his antlers.

"I'm sorry about this," I told him, as I pulled his head back and sliced through his jugular with the knife. Blood spewed out and filled the little bay. I had never seen so much blood in my life.

"It's better this way," I told him in a low, calm tone. "Otherwise, it might take you two or three days to die, with coyotes chewing on you while you're still alive. You deserve better than that. You are king of the forest. I'm going to turn off all the pain."

His eyes rolled back in his head, and still the blood poured from his neck. When he was finally dead, I pulled him onto the shore. His body would feed the coyotes, ravens, magpies, and crows.

As I squished up the rocky slope of the beach in my soaked, felt-lined boots, my face was warm, and not just from the exertion.

"I couldn't let him suffer anymore," I told Aaron, whose face was frozen in a look of horror and revulsion.

"We put him out of his misery," I said, more to myself than anyone else.

The memory of the little bay filled with blood came back into my mind. "I couldn't leave him like that," I croaked to myself, barely louder than a whisper.

I needed my father that day. The Point is a tough parish to run on my own.

INHERITANCE

Like Jesus, my father told stories to illustrate his sermon points. He also told them while fishing from his stone bench at the lake. To the common saying, "you can lead a horse to water, but you can't make him drink," he added the line, "but you can salt the hay." I can still see him saying this, with an index finger raised. He was imparting vital information. He always found anecdotes or recounted true events to hammer home or illustrate any point he was trying to make.

When we were children, we would accompany him through the gauntlet of three church services every Sunday. In one sermon, he told the story of a king who had the women of his nation cut their hair, to braid ropes, to move stones, to build a monument to himself. At the third service, after hearing the sermon twice, one of my sisters said to the other, "I'm tired; I'm going to take a little nap. Wake me up for the hair part." We've laughed about that for years.

The worst part was not that we had to listen to the same sermon three times. That was okay. Sometimes your mind would wander. Hearing the sermon three times was good for us. We daydreamed about God, which can never hurt.

The worst part of the Sunday ordeal was getting invited for supper at one of the parishioners' homes, between the afternoon service and the evening service. Fast food was not an option, and we rarely ate at restaurants, but we did need to eat something. We dreaded eating other people's strange food.

Over time, we developed various survival strategies. We took small portions to begin with, or secreted inedible food into a napkin and disposed of it in the toilet. Soft food, like mashed potatoes or creamed peas, made me gag, so I avoided those at all costs.

Being wary was a family trait. As we stood together in the cold November wind and stared at our floats on the water, my father told me about our family history. Between bites, my father told me about my grandfather, the farmer, and great-grandfather the teacher, and how the Russians had broken their promises, and had nearly killed them all in prison for the crime of being capitalists. My grandfather learned to have a healthy disrespect for government in general, and for the Russian government in particular.

In jail, the men of my family were treated much worse than animals. My grandfather Jacob (or Yasha, as they called him) grew very sick. It looked like he was going to die. That's when my great-grandfather George told one of my great-uncles that Yasha was not looking too good and would probably not make it through the night.

"Take Yasha's boots off," my great-grandfather said to my great-uncle. "They will be impossible to get off once he is dead."

Times were tough. Boots were boots. George was a practical man, a teacher. He didn't want to see boots go to waste.

Jacob, however, was alert enough to be aware of this conversation about his imminent death. He protested in the only way he could. He stiffened his feet so his boots could not be removed.

His brother struggled but was unable to remove the boots.

George was not to be deterred. In a voice filled with sadness and regret, in a time when children, even adult children, listened to their parents, he said one word to Jacob.

"Yasha." It was admonition and despair, under a ton of practicality.

Jacob relaxed his feet, and his boots were removed. Jacob obeyed his father, as he was expected to. But somewhere under that, the Rath stubbornness, was alive and well.

Jacob did not want to die. He refused to die. He made up his mind that he would not die.

He made it through the night, and the following days, and began to grow stronger. He recounted tales about the food they brought them, which sometimes had fleas floating on top of the broth. Jacob saved those for last, knowing he needed the protein.

In the stories our father told us, we learned how the Russian government had betrayed us. Our family has held this belief for more than

300 years. You see, Catherine the Great had invited hard-working Germans to homestead in Russia. My ancestors had been living in the Black Forest, where they had been grave diggers and blacksmiths, so the prospect of land, religious freedom, and exemption from conscription was appealing. They settled near Odessa, on the Black Sea. They had farms, with orchards and hired help.

It was just when my grandfather was about to fulfill the terms of settlement and own his land free and clear that the promises were broken. While he was away serving in the Russian army, his house was looted, the windows and doors taken. My grandmother, with a five-year-old child, trembled with fear when the soldiers came, shook a rifle in her face, and took what they wanted.

My grandfather was certain the Russians would come and find him in Canada. He was so certain of it that he passed that fear to my father, who slept with a rifle under his bed until the day he died. It doesn't matter that he had no bullets for the .303 British, a modified sporting version of a rifle used in the Second World War. Some hunters believe that the .303 British has killed more moose and deer than any other calibre rifle, just because there were so many of them after the war. We had one with notches carved into the stock – one for each moose it had killed.

Against this tapestry of my ancestors, I inherited a stubborn streak and put it to good use. I did this more than I should have.

There has been a George Rath in my family for generations. When it came time for me to name my son, I rebelled against "George." I simply refused. No one was going to change my mind. It was not so much the name that I protested, but that the family should be able to dictate how I named my children. I was above such things. I would not be bound by such silly traditions. I was my own man.

Of course, no man is an island unto himself. I am just a thread in a tapestry that stretches back hundreds of years. But I was not thinking about that when I chose names for my own sons, who are also part of that tapestry, whether they want to be or not. I named my sons Jonathan Paul and Aaron James.

I let Dan have the opportunity to pass the name forward. After all, he was Daniel George, and *he* should have been the one to pass that legacy down anyway. He rebelled, too, though, and did not name either of his sons George.

I was stubborn and foolish. I cannot speak for my brother's actions. Perhaps he'll explain them to his sons someday.

Time passed. My rebellion was forgotten. My sons were accepted into the family – even though neither one of them had a George in their name. My sons grew up. I now have a grandson named George. Someday, I will take George to the Point. Between fish, we will talk about our place in the tapestry, about my father Ernest, my grandfather Jacob, and my great-grandfather George.

The fact that my father kept a gun didn't mean he liked hunting. My father did *not* like hunting or killing anything, except ants. My father had a specific hatred of ants. I told him once that whenever I killed a bug in the garden, I said a prayer, asking God to forgive me for taking this life, but that I had to. It was in the wrong place. My father looked at me, bemused, and said that he hated ants, and danced on their heads.

He did go moose hunting, mind you, but he never actually killed anything. He once had to slit the throat of a deer that had been shot by his partner. Later, he recalled the event in such graphic detail, saying it felt like slicing the throat of his own child, that just hearing the story prevented me from hunting for years.

I cannot imagine what my father thought he would do with that gun, but it gave him some comfort. When someone kicks your door open in the middle of the night, it is never good news. You don't get over something like that. My grandfather passed that fear to my father, who passed it on to me.

I can't shake it. It's not the monster that lives under my bed that I fear. It is not the rifle I keep there. It's not even the thought of the Russian secret police breaking down my door in the middle of the night and dragging me off to some unfathomable existence. What troubles me is that unspeakable things have been etched on my ancestral DNA.

Things for which there is no cure. I wake groggy and spent, worn out from trying to scrub off these memories, which is like trying to de-contaminate radiation I have been exposed to for generations. To es-cape, I fish.

HONOUR

I do not remember seeing a gun prior to my arrival in Canada, although I must have seen them both in Brazil and in the U.S. I certainly knew what they were, but perhaps that was from TV. Three incidents stand out in my mind concerning guns. Two took place on my grandfather's farm in southern Alberta. The other took place under a rising moon.

First, the farm. When my grandfather Jacob got off the boat in St. John, New Brunswick, he bought a ticket on the train as far as the money he had would take him and his small family. He landed in Rosebud, Alberta, with a five-year-old son, a pregnant wife, and five dollars left in his pocket.

He made his living by butchering and sausage-making for the farmers in the community. His German fastidiousness, his penchant for cleanliness, and his work ethic earned him a reputation as the man to get to help with butchering. The meat he cut, and the sausage he made in those early days, fed his family.

I have my grandfather's .22 rifle, which he acquired along the way and used to dispatch his own pigs and cows. I remember him butchering a pig to make sausage, with the head, scrubbed clean, sitting in a tub to make head cheese. Nothing was wasted. A single bullet hole, the smooth dark edges stark against the neon pinkness of the rest of the skin. The inside of the hole a deep hue of red. Such a small hole to create so much blood.

The gun did not pass to my father first. It came straight to me. The rifle is a bolt action, single shot .22 calibre Cooey. It came with rust on the barrel, the stock in need of refinishing, and the front sight bent alarmingly to the right. I refinished the stock, scoured the rust from the barrel, and re-blued it. I had the sight replaced and thought I would give the gun to my grandson – something from his great-great-grandfather.

The boy's mother, a vegan, is okay with the idea of the weapon, as long as it is not used to harm any animals. Paper targets are fine. For me, that's okay. The .22 is more a toy than a tool. I have no livestock to butcher. Without telescopic sights, the gun is not useful for bird hunting, and its single-shot action makes it slow to operate at the range. It is a toy for me, a connection to my grandfather, for whom it *was* a tool.

My father, however, had not needed a scope the day he showed the gun to me. The .22 slouched unattended in a corner of the chop house. This was long before any safe firearms storage regulations were even thought of, let alone instated and enforced. The .22 rifle was like a pitchfork or a hammer. It was nothing special.

The chop house was a building next to the barn. A machine, which attached to the power take-off of the tractor, ground grain into a fine powder for use as animal feed. The chop house was a good place to find mice and smelled of grain and dust. Everything was coated with dust as fine as flour.

"Show me how it works," I said, trembling, unable to mask my excitement. "Shoot something!"

My father grabbed the rifle, fumbled with a cardboard box of shells, selected one with his thick fingers, and put a round in the chamber. Four sparrows sat on the very peak of the pig barn's swayback roof, enjoying the cool morning air. My father took aim at one of them.

He was either a crack shot or very lucky. At the sharp blast of sound, which echoed back to us from the surrounding buildings, three sparrows took off in flight. One did not fly. It fell forward, almost drunkenly, in slow motion. Moving but not alive, it began to roll slowly down the roof, picking up speed as it neared the bottom. Then it seemed to be flying, but it was still falling, not really flying. I willed it to fly with all my heart. The bird did not fly but came to rest abruptly on the top of the manure pile, with a soft thud.

I was amazed at my father's ability – excited and ashamed all at once. I had encouraged him. I thrilled at the power of the weapon, but was ashamed at the senselessness of the death, and that I had caused it. Those feelings swirled around me in a tsunami of emotion. We never spoke of that incident again.

The second memory of my encounter with a gun was with a 12-gauge shotgun, which was stored behind the door of the milk house. The milk house was a building close to the farmhouse where the milk separator was kept. After the cows were milked in the barn, the milk was brought here and run through the milk separator to extract the cream. The milk was then put into metal cans, which were picked up and trucked to the dairy. Milk for drinking was also prepared in the milk house. Skim milk, which was left over from the separating process, was used to feed the animals. My grandfather also made his own "sour milk." It had clumps in it, and both my father and grandfather loved it.

The shotgun stood behind the milk room door. My grandfather had once used it to kill a lynx that was in a tree behind his garden. He skinned the lynx and made a rug out of the hide. After that, it lay on the floor in my father's old room, where I slept when we visited.

My sisters slept in the adjoining room, which had a double bed with an iron headboard. I primed them with tales that at night, when the moon was full, the lynx fur would come to life and would certainly devour them. Then, after the lights were off, I would throw the rug on my back and growling and snarling, leap onto their bed, causing them to scream in utter terror, which brought the full attention of my father, who bounded up the stairs in a flash to see what all the commotion was about. There were consequences, of course, for the screaming, and I may not have received my fair share for being the instigator of the event.

On the day in question, I was taught the valuable lesson of not pointing guns at people. I don't remember exactly how old I was – perhaps nine or ten. I vividly remember standing with the shotgun at my hip, pointing it at my grandfather who was approaching the milk house. This was an old 12-gauge single-shot break action shotgun. Somehow, I had managed to get the stiff hammer in the cocked position. My finger was on the trigger. "Stick 'em up, Grandpa," I said. My grandfather who was in mid-stride at the time, froze. He was less than ten feet away from where I was standing. The milk house was two steps up from the ground, and the result was the gun was pointed squarely at my grandfather's chest.

At this point, my father, who was working on something close by, became aware of the dangerous situation unfolding around him. My father was calm, but there was an unnatural tone of urgency in his voice – a bleating quiver that was not normally there. He told me that what I was doing was extremely dangerous. I remember clearly my father telling me to not pull the trigger, and to put the gun down. My finger was on the trigger, the gun was cocked. A gun is designed for a finger to fit into the trigger guard and then onto the trigger. I had been clearly told to not pull the trigger. I *had* to pull the trigger. I pulled the trigger.

Fortunately, there was nothing but a loud click. Had the gun been loaded, I certainly would have killed my grandfather. My grandfather came and took the shotgun away from me, and my father explained to me in great, graphic detail about how vital it is not to point guns at people – *ever*.

Needless to say, it was a lesson I never forgot. It was one of the fundamental lessons about guns that my father taught me that day. Never point guns at people. Ever, EVER, *EVER!* And when told not to pull the trigger, it is best to comply with that request as well.

It was years later when I had my own shameful experience with a gun and a bird. I can't remember what I promised to my parents that convinced them to let me buy a pellet gun, but eventually I wore them down. It was a Czechoslovakian-made, spring-loaded break-action air rifle.

It was spring or early summer. A robin stood on the circle of logs we had used to make a skating rink in the winter. I shot at the robin. I hit the robin.

I did not kill it. Its wing was broken. I went after it, shooting, and missing, and shooting again. I knew that I couldn't leave him injured. I followed him across the yard into the trees.

Sometimes a robin will display a broken wing to lead a predator away from the nest. This robin was not pretending.

Eventually I caught up with him and finished him off. I was ashamed. This shooting was a stupid, senseless act, and it bothered me deeply. I could see the robin hunch over in death, and I put one more pellet into him to be sure. My mouth was full of ashes. I vowed to myself not to kill anything ever again that I was not going to eat. I have kept that promise.

The third incident happened years later. Before I get to it, though, I should explain that I often went with my father as he hunted moose. On these treks through the bush I carried my grandfather's 12-guage shot gun, which is *not* a moose gun. I wanted to shoot a "chicken." That's what we called grouse. My father said no. He always said no. He said the sound of the shot would scare the moose away. Every time we went hunting. Every time I asked. He said no. I told him it was better to go home with a grouse or two rather than nothing, but he never let me shoot a grouse. We always went home with nothing.

My hunting buddies were of the same mind as my father, also setting their sights on bigger game. If they drove by a ruffed grouse, my favourite, standing on the edge of the road, they'd always say, "Sorry, Rath." It became an inside joke. Those guys delighted in tormenting me. (And why was the ruffed grouse standing by the road, you ask? To eat gravel – of course! – to help crush its diet of kinnickinnick berries, its favourite food.)

Of course, the year I drew the magic ticket, the draw of a lifetime, a 6-point bull elk, they had to be nice to me. That year, they let me shoot every grouse we saw. That was the fall my first wife left. Over the course of the fall, I was in the bush more than 20 days, licking my wounds. Along the way to find the bull elk, we shot an immature bull moose, a bear, and about 50 grouse, but nothing had prepared me for the feelings of remorse I felt standing over the carcass of the bull elk I had spent weeks looking for.

Some hunters, the honest ones, will talk about "shooter's remorse." As an adult and as a hunter, I have often felt the full effects of it, though never so powerfully as that evening I stood over the warm body of that magnificent elk, steam rising off him in the newly risen moonlight, asking myself "What have I done?"

Not long after that, I was in a classroom in Rigaud, Quebec, being taught about firearms by someone who did not have the benefit of my father's instruction. There were a dozen people in the class. We formed a semi-circle around the instructor. I was immediately to his right. Across from me one of my classmates formed the other arm of the horseshoe. The instructor was describing and pointing out the various parts of long guns. He grabbed a rifle off the table and began describing and naming the various parts: butt, stock, action, muzzle, etc. I began to squirm. The barrel of the gun was pointed directly at my chest. I know the firearm was deactivated, but I tried to move out of the line of fire, nonetheless.

The instructor then flipped the rifle upside down to show us the trigger, the trigger guard, etc., and pointed the muzzle directly in the centre of my classmate's chest. I was quite shocked that the instructor would be so careless. All I could think was that he was fortunate that my father was not present, or he might have received some remedial gun-handling instruction.

It was years later, another gun course, my employer's insistence that I carry a gun at work and actually point it at people, and damage to my left knee that helped to end my work for Canada Customs at the border. These days, my damaged knee keeps me from hunting. I shot some ptarmigan one fall, but after cooking them up, decided they tasted like liver, not like the wonderful white meat of ruffed grouse, so I leave the little white birds alone.

My rifles, along with the .22 from my grandfather, destined for my grandson when he gets a little older, are locked away, stored securely according to regulations, awaiting their chance to get to the range and make some noise. There is nothing quite like the smell of gunpowder after a gun has been fired, especially in the crisp air of a fall morning. Paper targets are just fine.

LIFE LESSONS

One of the lessons I have had difficulty learning over the years is the one about choosing forgiveness instead of revenge. I can still hear my father's voice quoting, "Vengeance is mine saith the Lord." He would have used the poetic language of the *King James Version*, but the New International Version is clearer:

If it is possible, as far as it depends on you, live at peace with everyone. Do not take revenge, my dear friends, but leave room for God's wrath, for it is written: "It is mine to avenge; I will repay," says the Lord.

On the contrary: "If your enemy is hungry, feed him; if he is thirsty, give him something to drink. In doing this, you will heap burning coals on his head." – Romans 12:18–20

Powerful stuff.

I glossed over the part about living at peace with everyone. I liked the part about heaping burning coals on the head of my enemy, though. It's not that I don't know the right way, and haven't been taught, or never had the correct behaviour modelled for me. But I also knew that God was pretty busy. I wanted to help out – by meting out some vengeance on my own, where warranted. I did *not* want to wait for God to take the time to settle accounts. My flesh cried out for vengeance. It still does, but I have sanded that little knot in my personality for more than 50 years, and it is slowly disappearing.

Neither my father nor my grandfather were vengeful people. When my grandfather had made the plan to come to Canada, he knew he would need some money. He asked his stepbrother to run an errand for him, to go to a widow with money, and ask her to lend my grandfather some money, which he would repay once he was established in Canada. When my grandfather told the story, it was a "hundred dollars." A hundred dollars was shorthand for a large sum of money.

When the stepbrother returned, my grandfather asked for the money, and was told solemnly that "she wouldn't give it." My grandfather was surprised and disappointed, but took it in stride and went to the new world without it.

He was shocked sometime later, though, when a letter from Russia arrived from the widow, reminding him of his promise and requesting payment of the loan. My grandfather realized that the stepbrother had betrayed him, taken the money and kept it for himself. What could he do? The widow had given the money in good faith, and though my grandfather did not have the benefit of it, he had to repay it. Did he hate the stepbrother? No. Did he seek vengeance? No. He forgave and moved on. But he had a story to tell.

I have a story to tell, too, but this one is about how I did *not* forgive and move on. As a supervisor at Canada Customs, I saw my role as a problem solver. It was my job to remove whatever barriers prevented my staff from doing their work. I took that role very seriously. My staff were protecting the homeland, and I was moving obstacles out of their way. Sometimes those obstacles consisted of a lack of training, or a lack of equipment. Sometimes the barrier was a lack of motivation, or the lack of diesel fuel for the vehicle. I tried to remove all the barriers that I could.

In one case, we had a credit card for the government vehicle. Not all gas stations accepted the card. One time, when we were out of town, we needed diesel. The only gas station in town would not accept the vehicle's designated gas card. I also had a government credit card in my wallet, called an acquisition card. It had a limit of $5,000 on it and was to be used to purchase supplies and equipment. There were strict rules about its use. One rule was no personal purchases.

Fair enough. Another was that the acquisition card could not under any circumstances be used for travel.

That, however, was a problem. We needed diesel to fuel our vehicle so we could return to our base of operations.

Simple. I was the supervisor. I removed that barrier by taking the acquisition card out of my wallet and buying gas with it, which was strictly forbidden. The barrier was removed, and we went on our way.

Months later, I received a series of e-mails and phone calls from the bean counter who monitored the use of my card. She told me that gas was not an authorized purchase and that I was in contravention of the card agreement. I calmly explained that the only gas station available to us had refused the vehicle's gas card. I stated I had no other reasonable alternative to get my team and equipment safely back home. (I could have used my personal credit card for the purchase, and then waited for months to get reimbursed, but I was unwilling to do that. Why should I as a private citizen pay expenses for the Government of Canada?) The brow-beating lecture continued and took on a decidedly nasty tone.

"I understand the policy," I said, "but if faced with the same circumstances in the future I will make the same decision."

She threatened me with the removal of my card and other sanctions.

I stopped listening. I decided that she had lost the right to communicate with me ever again, as long as we both should live. I made a rule in my e-mail that any communication from her would be placed directly in the "Trash" folder.

In the end, it was win-win. We are now both retired. We don't need to talk. We don't.

SAINT MATTRESS

There is no truth to the accusation that I sometimes sat in the front row at church and covertly tried to make the candles on the altar flicker, just with my breath. None at all. Preposterous.

My father's sermons were structured, and usually contained two themes: "the Law" and the gospel. The Law showed us that humans are by nature sinful, have fallen short, and deserve the wrath of God. The gospel was the good news that we could be right with God. There would also be a part about salvation, which was provided free.

Dad's pastoral message was that heaven could not be obtained under one's own steam. I realized that you can't make candles flicker from the front row. We weren't so far from each other, really.

To Pastor Rath, good works counted for nothing. A sermon, though, counted for a lot. It had three parts: the goal (an explication of a text from scripture), the malady (whatever sin was separating us from God that day), and the means (how we could resolve the problem). There were scriptures relating to each part, and illustrations to drive the point home.

I tended to get lost in the candle flame. I was hopeless – and out of breath.

After church, around the dining room table, my father always asked us what the day's sermon had been about. We were like novices in a seminary.

It was advisable to take notes during the service. Dan and I never did. My sister Rose *always* took notes. She made us look bad, especially when we rolled our eyes and tried our best to derail our father.

"What was the sermon about, children?" asked Pastor Dad.

"God," I said. Sometimes Dan said it. We were like an echo. Or a dog pack.

Technically, our answer was true, but it was also not the answer my father was looking for. Whatever it was, we were sure we could bluff our way through it as well.

"What else?" he prompted.

"Sin," I said. Dan nodded. Or I nodded sagely as *he* said, "Sin."

Also technically true, but a game like this could go on forever. Actually, that was our goal.

Rose didn't see the point in that. She played this power game differently, biding her time, almost vibrating with excitement to provide the right answers.

But not yet. We were still in the spotlight.

"What *about* sin?" Dad asked, far from exasperated, but noticeably tiring of the game. Our victorious smirks must have seemed childish to him Still, he had a very long fuse.

"God doesn't like it," Dan would offer – that is, if I didn't say, "He's totally against it," first.

It was at this delicate juncture that Rose could no longer hold back. She swooped in to save the day, reciting the theme of the sermon, outlining each of the three parts, and relating them to the applicable scripture passages. Compared to our generic non-answers, she looked like a rock star.

Perfect. Dan and I sat and looked like angels of chagrin and awe, secretly grateful and gleeful that we had once again successfully avoided the detection of our lack of listening skills. Or so we thought.

Dad never skipped church. Other than when he was sick, he didn't do it; but even then he had to be *really* sick. Even if we were on holidays, far from our normal routine, we would find ourselves on a Sunday morning, worshipping in another Lutheran church of the appropriate synod. No exceptions.

As we grew older and sometimes had to work, we could cut church and get away with it. Work was the best excuse. Not really a good excuse, because it clearly went against the Third Commandment, but my father reluctantly accepted it. He instinctually knew if we were not being truthful, though. He would then ask us if we had gone to "Saint Mattress." This was code.

Lutherans are not Catholics and are aware of that fact. Five hundred years ago, Martin Luther made a point of challenging the Catholic church, which at the time was making a tidy profit by charging people for the forgiveness of sins. Luther was incensed, and Lutherans have been incensed for the past 500 years, just on that one point alone.

Because we were as frail and sinful as any other people, though, we looked down upon the Catholics. In fact, we referred to sleeping in on Sunday morning as going to "Saint Mattress." This was disrespectful on so many levels yet was also a rich vein of gold for promoting our supposed superiority over the Catholics.

The expression joined two prejudices: a general Lutheran dislike of saints, and a mockery of the Mass said in Latin. In our way of thinking, because the average Catholic in the pew didn't know what was being said during Mass, attending it had to have about the same effect as staying in bed. They might as well have stretched out on the pew. It wasn't very kind of us, but don't get us started on the pope. How could any single, imperfect man be infallible?

We were proud, I'll give you that. The sport of looking down upon the Catholic church was second only to our derision of liberal churches. In the opinion of most Lutherans we knew, liberal churches, including liberal Lutherans, had thrown out so much that nothing good was left.

I enticed Dad to attend Saint Mattress once. We didn't exactly sleep in, though. We got up very early. The plan was to travel to Vancouver, spend the night with my sister Kathy, catch a hockey game, then take the ferry to Vancouver Island, drive to Port Alberni to Brian's place, my first wife's brother, fish for three days, then return home. The rub, at least for Dad, was that we would have to skip church. We didn't *have* to skip church, but if we were going all that way for such a short time, we wanted to maximize our time on the river. I hoped God would understand.

Dad was torn. He wanted to experience salmon fishing on the river. I told him that catching a 30-pound fish in the river, where the current could catch it like a sail, was an experience not to be missed.

On the night we arrived, we lay in bed, looking up at the stars through the skylights. We tried to sleep but could not. At one point, I asked Dad if he was too excited to sleep, and he answered that he was.

It seemed that we had stared at the stars for hours. We were supposed to get up at 5 a.m., have breakfast, make our lunch, then set out to be on the river at first light, but we were out of bed and dressed at 3 a.m. making ham and cheese sandwiches with a good dose of mustard to help them slide down.

We drove to the pool on the Somass River in the dark, arriving an hour before first light. Someone was camped near the pool in a pickup and camper. They were still in bed when we drove up. We saw them open the door in their long johns to find out what was going on. We waved. We also got to choose the best spot on the river.

As we stood along the rocks on the shore waiting for first light, we heard the fish leaping out of the water and splashing back down. We squinted into the gloom but could not see them. Our excitement built minute by minute, until we could hardly bear it. We waited 45 minutes in real time, which was days in waiting time, until there was enough light to see the float, or enough light to sometimes see the float.

We had a great day. That year the rains were late and the salmon were milling about in the bay waiting for the water in the river to rise. Some of them were dark. We called them stove pipes. That is how dark they were. Not exactly bright as a piece of chrome, which is how you usually think of salmon. Some people on the river that day kept whatever they caught, but I was more fussy, releasing the darker fish and keeping only the bright ones. Many were over 30 pounds.

We wore chest waders and were in the river with the fish, the current pushing against us as we navigated the slippery rocks. Once something nudged me. I looked down in the clear water to see a huge fish bumping into my leg. It was about 30 pounds, but with the magnification of the water looked huge – like it could chew my leg off.

After three days of fishing, I was exhausted. I wanted a shower and a beer, and to sit and rest my aching back. My father wanted to continue fishing.

I left him there, got cleaned up and returned, finally, hours later. He was still fishing in the same place. If you were fishing with my dad, you had to pack dynamite to blow him off the water so you could go home.

Finally, we arrived back at Kathy's place in Vancouver.

"Where did you go to church?" she asked, in her direct way. It was a reasonable question. There was no reasonable alternative within the realm of possibility. My father always went to church.

Dad and I looked at each other. There was a pause.

"Saint Somass," I replied.

"Is that a Catholic church?" she asked, hardly daring to believe we had gone to a Catholic church.

"Not sure," I answered, "but the benches were hard as rocks."

"The message was deep," said my father joining in, "shallow in some places, but deep, very deep, in others."

Kathy began to catch on as we continued.

"The message had a lot of 'meat' in it," Dad said.

"I see," Kathy said, having trouble comprehending a world where my father had cut church to go fishing. That was even worse than going to Saint Mattress. She shook her head in disbelief.

I just smiled. Beatifically.

SHARING THE PEACE

Around the time I had secured my freedom and independence by earning my driver's licence, my father encouraged all of his children to attend other churches. We knew what he was up to and for the most part resisted. He was not at all suggesting that he wanted us to experience other versions of the Christian faith, or even other faiths. Far from it. He wanted us to check out the competition.

It's not that other Christian churches were competition, spiritually. What my father wanted was a sense of what others were doing in a practical way. Did we feel welcome or left to ourselves? Was there a bulletin? Did people talk to us? Was there any technique that he could incorporate into his own services? We were spies.

"Some churches have specific families assigned to take any visitors home with them for a meal," my father said. "Not in some nebulous future, but right now. Good idea! This makes people feel welcome, and they form a relationship with the host family. Smart."

We were too shy and self-conscious to be any use at taking notes, although from time to time I did find myself in a different church. It was only when I was an adult that I got into the swing of it.

Once, I was in a Catholic church in one of Rio's favelas. The church sat 365 steps up, on the top of a hill. I was using a crutch because of an injured knee. The funicular was not working. It was as hot as an oven, but our host wanted us to experience this particular church on the top of this particular hill. The steps were short and wide, and spaced in such a way that each step interrupted my stride. It was like walking the ties of a railroad track, with the complication of stepping upwards. Perhaps the steps were engineered this way so the faithful could say a prayer on each step. I sweltered on my way up, while Lisa scampered ahead like a gazelle.

The church was beautiful and the view of Rio stunning. As I rested my knee for the 365 steps that waited patiently for my return, I saw a young man with a bundle of brooms and mops on his shoulder. I asked our host what the young man was doing and learned that he was going to sell the brooms and mops in the favela and had come here to pray before going out to do his work. I reached into my pocket and pulled out $10.

"You want to buy a broom?" my guide asked me incredulously.

"No," I replied. "I think his devotion and faith should be rewarded."

The three of us struggled with the language barrier but, at the top of the stairs, our guide, the young man with the brooms, and an out-of-shape tourist leaning on his cane and sweating profusely reached a workable understanding of faith, devotion, and the 365 stairs to where the car was parked.

The most memorable Catholic church I have been in, though, or rather the most memorable experience I have had in a Catholic church, was a humble church in Kelowna, not a cathedral lined with gold.

The young priest that day wore a full, bushy beard and was dressed in a brown cassock tied at the waist. To me, he looked like a friar out of Robin Hood's forest, or how I imagined one would look, or how movies have taught me to believe a friar might have looked. He greeted us with a voice my father would have described as "being able to sing basso profundo in a Russian choir."

In my dad's church, we "shared the peace" at the communion service on the first Sunday of each month. My dad said to the congregation, "The peace of the Lord be with you always," and the congregation responded by saying, "And also with you." Then the members of the congregation were invited to share the peace with each other.

In most churches I have been in, you turn and shake hands with people within reach, and say, "Peace be with you." The appropriate response is, "And also with you." Some people are too shy to give the response; some don't wait for your response and are in a hurry to share the peace with someone else. Some say nothing at all and just stare at you solemnly as you shake their hand.

I have been in churches where the sharing of the peace is not so controlled. Actually, pandemonium breaks out. Everyone wants to share the peace with everyone else, which can be problematic for those who sit at the front and who are trying to shake the hand of those sitting at the back. The kids get into the act, and for five minutes total mayhem ensues. It is a good mayhem, but foreign to my measured Lutheran sensibilities.

In the Catholic church that day, the priest began sharing the peace. He left the chancel area and stepped down to where the congregation, who were now standing, was located. The priest shook hands with those sitting on the aisle for the first four or five rows. "Peace be with you. Peace be with you. Peace be with you." Then he stopped, made a sweeping gesture with his right hand to all the rest of us, and said, "And with you all." He delivered this blessing in his basso profundo voice, which filled the humble church from front to back and echoed off the back walls and back to the chancel. It was an all-consuming and all-enveloping wave of sound.

This blessing had a profound effect on me. The sharing of the peace had always been one of my favourite parts of worship – perhaps because of its built-in sense of community – and here it was, vibrant and overwhelming, and in a Catholic church. The hairs stood up on the back of my neck and I had a tingling sensation running down my head and shoulders to my mid-back. It was like I was receiving the peace in a spiritually and physically tangible manner.

I don't remember anything else about the service, or what the priest said. I have shared the peace in many churches, including my own, but I have never experienced that tingling spiritual effervescence again.

As I said, I was a poor spy. I never reported this occurrence to my father. We could talk about anything at the Point, but not this. I was unable to risk sharing this deeply personal and inexplicable experience with him, and having it minimized. No doubt, I mentioned the priest and his voice, perhaps even the Russian choir, but the rest I have kept to myself.

Now I'm sharing this peace with you.

The peace of the Lord be with you always.

WHISKEY

During the summers, when white fish do not run, we chased land-locked salmon, called kokanee. We fished for them in Okanagan Lake at Okanagan Centre, near the water intake for the Hiram Walker distillery over the mountain in Winfield. That's what we were told. Hiram Walker distilled whiskey there in those days and aged it in charred oak barrels. That we knew.

A friend of mine, Mark, bought a couple of used barrels from the distillery to make swish. Swish is made by pouring a gallon of water into the barrel and rotating it a little each day. The whiskey which has soaked into the charcoal and oak barrel is absorbed into the water. After a week or so, you get almost a gallon of swish. It is similar to whiskey, but costs only the price of the barrel.

Mark took one of his barrels apart to see how it was made but then could not reassemble it. After he gave up, I bought both barrels from him to cut in half and make planters, because I liked puzzles.

Reassembling the whiskey barrel was a challenge. I thought I could match the staves to each other if I followed the pattern the metal bands had made on the oak. It was a good theory. Each stave had a notch near each end in which the top and bottom of the barrel fit respectively. My problem was that I needed to match the staves to each other, place them around the lid and bottom, then hold everything together with the metal bands. I had three sets of arms less than I needed. Eventually I got it together, not in the original configuration, but close enough that by running water in it for a week, the staves swelled up and held water.

Whiskey does strange things to men. When we neared the fabled water intake, my father always spit into the water. "In case it makes it into the whiskey," he said.

I didn't understand it then, and I don't really understand it now. Perhaps Dad did it because one of our fishing teachers, Alvin (also a pastor), modelled the behaviour. Who knows what Dad's motivation was? Perhaps he thought it was funny that his spit would end up in the whiskey. I didn't.

Alvin's motivation was obvious. Alvin was retired and had an old-school wooden boat that smelled of fish and gasoline. He critiqued my father's sermons and was a burr under my father's saddle. He spoke with the high-pitched voice of a man whose stomach had stretched his vocal cords taut. He was quick to point out fault in others, but not too keen to hear about his own shortcomings.

Long before photocopiers became commonplace, every church had a mimeograph machine for printing bulletins, annual reports, Bible studies, and the like. These devices were similar to a miniature printing press. A stencil made of a thin plastic material was cut by the keys on a typewriter, then was placed on the mimeograph machine – backwards. Ink came through the stencil, neatly transferring the printed words to paper, the right way around.

It was a finicky machine, though. Ink had to be applied correctly and in the right place and in the right amount. The ink was not fast drying, either, so it was possible to get some bleed from one page to the next, and on your hands.

One day, Dad and I were at the church when Alvin and his wife were printing their Christmas letter in the mimeograph room. Alvin had typed the letter on a stencil and was printing it on special Christmas paper. It was not going well. He was getting frustrated.

Alvin's wife was a sweet, kind-hearted woman named Louise. As Alvin was fussing with the machine, she began to recount a story about when Alvin had forced the stencil on the wrong way, causing the words to be printed backwards.

"He tried to wipe off the thick ink," she said, "and ended up not only making a mess but having to re-do the stencil." She wasn't laughing. She was just innocently recounting the story.

Alvin stared at her over his glasses with a withering look. "There are bats in the belfry," he scolded her, "and there needs to be an extermination."

She stopped her story mid-sentence, her mouth opened slightly, then clamped shut in a straight line. He had spoken.

I was reading recently that all the water we have on the planet has been used many times. Not to put too fine a point on it, but that means the water we are now drinking has a history – and it is possible it was also used by the dinosaurs. So the molecules in water we are now drinking were previously consumed and voided by dinosaurs. Talk about peeing in the well!

It also means that some of the water molecules the dinosaurs drank and peed in were also in the lake, and in the whiskey, and in Alvin and in the fish and in us, all with their own stories to tell.

The stories the lake can tell! And fish swim through them all! And we catch the fish!

See what I mean about fishermen contemplating the secrets of the universe? I'll leave that for you to ponder the next time the ice is clinking in your glass. *Na zdrowie!*

LAKE WHITE FISHING

At 74, Albert had 50 years on me. He came complete with a pacemaker, a backpack, and a log peavey made of aluminum. Albert had agreed to take me fishing for lake white fish, which could be found in the waters under the log booms on Westside Road. For *that,* I needed a peavey.

The peavey looked more like a whale harpoon than a log handling tool. It had a long handle, a sharp-pointed spear at the business end, and, perpendicular to that, a curved hook, also with a pointed end. It was used on the log booms to pull bundles of logs close enough to jump from one to another.

A boom is a jumble of log bundles, each the size of a logging truck and kept in place by boom sticks – single logs chained together to form a pen to keep the bundles from floating away.

"The bundles aren't always stable," Albert explained. "They can flip over without warning. The wind can push the bundles away from shore as far as the boom sticks will allow."

Lake white fish are the cousins of mountain white fish. They look as though a mountain white fish has been inflated to three or four times normal size. They are plumper than the sleek fish I was used to catching, but oddly had the same-sized heads. They had the reputation for being excellent smoked, and because of the larger size the bones were also larger and more easily dealt with. I was excited.

The sky was grey that morning, with high cloud diffusing the light. The water along the log booms was troubled by the wind and formed a patina of little riffles. The water between the log bundles, however, was dark and still.

We disregarded the "No Trespassing" and "Danger Keep Off" signs and climbed onto the booms. Albert was as spry as a young goat, and as sure-footed. He jumped from bundle to bundle, rod in one hand, log peavey in the other to augment his footing, the rest of his gear in a rucksack on his back. Several times he had to wait for me to catch up as I struggled clumsily behind.

When we came to the boom sticks, Albert gave me special instructions. "Boom sticks are not large enough to hold your weight," he said. "You have to step down from a log bundle onto a boom stick, which will go under water, then onto the next boom stick, which will also go under water, then up onto the next log bundle."

The idea churned my stomach. It seemed impossible. How could you stand on something that would not hold your weight, move on to something else that would not hold your weight, and climb onto an unpredictable log bundle? This was like church. A slippery concoction at best.

It was November and the water was cold. Getting wet was the least of our potential problems. The log bundles could move and we could find ourselves under water, under a log bundle, looking for the sky, weighted down with our heavy clothing. It seemed like a recipe for disaster.

Albert noticed the fear in my eyes and broke the procedure down for me patiently.

"Step lightly onto the first boom stick," he said, "but keep moving. Once the log goes under water and bounces back up, you will already be on the second boom stick. Keep moving. When it starts to go under the water, you will already be climbing onto the next log bundle."

When I still looked like a goat facing God's wrath, he said, "Think of the boom sticks as burning rocks. If you stay for more than a second, you'll get burned."

"Burned?" I asked, remembering that the Good Book says, *"Thou shalt not covet thy fishing partner's peavey."*

Albert demonstrated. His feet were light. He danced across the boom sticks and stood on a log bundle, smiling at me. Well, if a guy in his 70s could do it?

I stepped down onto the first boom stick, my clumsy feet made of cement and lead. Bile rose up in the back of my throat. I tasted my fear.

As promised, the boom stick dove to the bottom of the lake. It was then that I remembered that I was not supposed to be there, and stepped awkwardly to the next boom stick, which also headed downwards, the water swirling to catch my foot, but I was already gone, reaching for Albert's hand as he helped me onto the next log bundle. I had survived the crossing of the boom sticks with only slight damage to my pride, and a hint of water at the bottoms of my boots.

We fished that day, using mealworms on a special homemade hook of Albert's design, which included copper wound around the hook shank. The lake white fish came to eat moss that grew under the log bundles. We were trying to convince them to eat our hooks instead. This was different than normal fishing.

By the close of the day, Albert had caught one lake white fish that weighed about five pounds. I had caught nothing. I'd had a hard time focusing on the fishing. The whole day I was thinking too much about the penalty of falling into the water and getting trapped under a log bundle, unable to find the light. I kept thinking about the boom sticks we had to navigate on our way back to the truck, and with only the one log peavey between us. I kept trying not to covet it.

I thought Albert would offer the fish to me. I had rehearsed this. I would have declined, of course, but the offer never came. I could see a mountain white fishing spot from the log booms. I had fished there several times. It was right beside the road. No peavey needed.

Years later Albert died on Wood Lake. The heart attack came while he was backing his boat and trailer into the lake. Not the best time for a heart attack. Distracted by the heart attack, he was unable to stop the vehicle, and backed into the water, until the engine finally stopped.

When I heard the news, I remembered how spry and active he had been, and how he had taken me trespassing on the log booms.

I wonder what became of the log peavey that had always kept him out of deep water, until the last, when the deep water took him, and his truck.

SUMMER WHITE FISH

I was selling life insurance at the time. It was the hardest, most heart-breaking work I have ever done. I had been lured in with the promise of unlimited earning potential. Indeed, it is true that there was no ceiling. There was, however, also no floor.

One day the phone rang. When I answered, an arson investigator introduced himself.

"I am investigating a suspicious fire," he said. "I found your business card at the scene."

I was confused. I didn't know what I could have to do with a suspicious fire. I passed my card out to people all the time. I ordered them in boxes of 500.

The investigator went on to explain that, miraculously, the card was intact and had only burned around the edges, making a decorative border. My name and contact info were perfectly fine. He commented that he had never seen anything like it.

The investigator told me that everything he was telling me was strictly confidential, that the fire was clearly suspicious, and most certainly arson. He told me the name of the person who owned the trailer involved in the arson investigation. The man was a single parent of a three-year-old daughter.

I remembered him immediately. We had talked about white fish. He had even taken me to his own special spot to catch white fish in the summer.

I felt a bad taste in my mouth remembering all this. The investigator asked me if I had placed an insurance policy on the man's daughter.

It was a fair question. There are good reasons for insuring children, not least the cost of burial expenses. Children die. It is rare, but it does happen. You can also buy guaranteed insurability so that if a child develops an illness later in life, they can still buy insurance at standard rates, regardless of any dangerous hobbies or high-risk occupations.

"No," I said. "I didn't sell him a policy, but I certainly would have mentioned the benefits."

The investigator wondered out loud if the man had bought a policy on his child's life, then had tried to kill the child for the insurance money.

"We actually didn't do any business together," I said. "I can attest to his unethical and unsavoury behaviour when it came to fishing, though."

"What do you mean?" asked the investigator. His voice had an eager tone.

I told him the summer white fish story. It's a story of being out of synch. For me, white fish were only available three weeks of the year, when they congregated to spawn on the rocky shores of Okanagan Lake in mid-November. I never saw them the rest of the year. Truthfully, I wasn't really looking for them at any other time, but when I heard about white fish being available in the summer, I got very excited. My potential client said he was catching white fish every day, and that he would take me.

I was overjoyed. This would be a new experience, catching white fish in *warm* weather. It opened up a whole new world of possibilities. I wouldn't have to fight the cold for the thrill of catching white fish. My fingers would not be numb when I baited my hook.

We arranged a time and place to meet: the channel that runs between Kalamalka Lake and Wood Lake in Oyama. I got there first. When he showed up, I asked about maggots.

"We're not using maggots," he said.

I was puzzled. For me, maggots were critical to catching white fish.

As it turned out, he was using a weighted treble hook, casting it into a school of white fish, and catching one by snagging it. I was aghast. This was neither a legal nor a sportsman-like way to fish.

This was not what I had envisioned, and I did not want to take part in fishing unethically. The regulations are clear that to be legally caught, a fish has to be caught by the mouth. Catching a fish by snagging it on the side or belly is horrible and illegal. It is one thing to catch a fish in this manner accidentally. Things happen.

I once foul-hooked a halibut in his belly. It was the biggest fight of my life. The charter operator was perplexed about the fight. He could see me struggling and said it must be a huge halibut, bigger than he had ever seen. Halibut can grow to be 300 pounds or more. He rigged a harpoon which was tied to a huge bladder. This was used to tire out large fish. He maintained his watch at the stern of the boat while I battled my fish. After what seemed like an eternity, I heard him say words that are forever burned into my memory: "Get the net." It was not a monster after all, but a medium sized halibut, hooked in his stomach, causing him to come through the water like a sail, with maximum drag. The regulations were clear – a foul-hooked fish was to be returned to the water immediately and released. We were not starving. This was not life or death. Back it went. What a waste of effort.

What this man was doing in Oyama was no accident, though, and I left the channel sickened with disappointment. The potential of catching summer fish in a short sleeve shirt with the sun shining on my face, which had been dangled so enticingly in front of me like a dancing teardrop hook, had been snatched away.

I told the investigator all the details. He thanked me for my time and asked if I wanted to have the business card with the perfectly burned border that had been retrieved from the fire.

"No thanks," I said. The promise of the potential earnings from selling life insurance, like the potential of summer white fish, turned out to be a big disappointment. I didn't need any reminders of that.

PAYING IT FORWARD

There's a wise saying it's good to pay attention to: "Do not trifle with a man who names his fishing rods. He has no time to discuss the weather." We named our fishing rods.

Many of the rods we fished with over the years were inherited from our fishing teachers. My father's rod "A-frame," for example, was a gift from Ephram. The name was apt, because A-frame was a construct, an improvisation of old-world bamboo and new-world dowel that sat at a jaunty angle, like an old man with a crooked back. The name of the rod also played on Ephram's name and was a way of remembering him. It also looked a bit like an A-frame house.

When A-frame was taken apart, his segments were tied together with a broken shoelace. This generation of men recycled everything.

For years, I searched sporting goods stores from Kelowna to Vancouver for a new rod of suitable length and flexibility – something that would honour Ephram and my other fishing teachers. One day while I was working at the border, I met some men who worked in a factory making bamboo fly rods. I was intrigued. These rods were built in segments and cost around $5,000 U.S. each. These guys couldn't afford the rods they were building, mind you, but they were allowed to purchase seconds – rods that had a slight imperfection and couldn't be sold for full price.

I wanted to have a look at these rods, so I asked them to unpack and display the goods they were importing and show me an example of a flaw. They pointed to a dot, the size of a freckle you might find on the back of your hand. This insignificant blemish, natural to the wood, turned a $5,000 rod into a $200 one. It was the people I met at the border that made the job worthwhile.

Although the rods were beautiful, and masterfully constructed, they were not the rods I was looking for. A-frame had a solid wooden handle, repurposed from a broom or a closet clothes rod. This handle had a hole at one end. A bolt pushed through the metal end of the bamboo rod was attached with a nut to the wooden handle. This improvisation gave A-frame the required length, and the less-than-eye-pleasing line. A-frame had the correct level of sentimental attachment, but to me, he lacked the flexibility of other rods. His wooden handle made him heavy, clumsy, and awkward. My father often sat on his favourite rock, the bishop's chair, with A-frame resting in his lap, jutting and lurching toward the lake at an alarming angle. It was just the way A-frame was. An amalgam, an oddity – a curiosity.

But A-frame could catch fish despite his appearance, and that's what I was looking for – a rod that knew what he was doing, that would make a good fishing partner, that wouldn't get in the way of my line, and that didn't require a nut. More than once, my Dad or I dropped A-frame's nut onto the rocks while tightening or loosening it, because our fingers were so cold. Sometimes we couldn't find it again.

A-frame was a pro, though. I often stood by as my father bounced fish off my stomach and into the ice-glazed pail. "Automatic de-hooking," Dad remarked with surprise and delight, when the fish spit out the hook and splashed into the pail.

I fished with Spindly: 14 feet of bamboo pole cut into lengths reinforced with metal connectors. Before I was trusted with that fine rod, I bought a blank from Clem, a sporting goods guy whom Dad liked. That was a strange process.

"Men who fish for white fish are the laziest fishermen in the world," said Clem. "They park their car beside the lake and fish out the window."

Before that experience, I had naively thought that someone who wanted money in his pocket would do better by not insulting those who fished white fish. Obviously not. I bought the blank.

The blank was about ten and a half feet long. The upper half had been forced through the lower half, and the bottom taped shut. I could fish with this thing, but not well, so I didn't give it a name. It was too short when extended, yet long and awkward when stowed.

There was a rule from the teachers which said that a new man should not fish with old bamboo. A beginner needed to learn some finesse before he could be trusted with one of these priceless, irreplaceable artifacts. So the blank rod it was. That thing served me, poorly, until one of the masters of white fishing died and I was given Spindly, who was no thicker at any of his segments than the diameter of my little finger, and whose tip was so thin and flexible that it bent nearly to the breaking point when landing a fish.

Over the years, Spindly had to be repaired in places with fibreglass, which spared his life, but stole some of his flexibility. That's why I was looking for a replacement.

After a long search, I found a 13-and-a-half-foot telescoping rod that I called Hawkeye. It had good flexibility, was easily flicked into action, and when stowed was shorter and easier to handle than any of the other rods. It is as black as deep, deep water.

I'm still looking for another bamboo rod, though. I will pass Spindly to my grandson George when he is ready. It won't be long now. He is almost as old now as his father was when I first took him to the Rock. He will learn with Hawkeye, I think, until he is ready to graduate to bamboo.

LITTLE RED HEN SYNDROME

In the folk story *The Little Red Hen,* a hen wants to bake some bread. She asks her neighbours for help to plant, water, and harvest the wheat, grind the wheat into flour, knead the dough, light the oven, shape the loaf, and bake the bread. None of the neighbours is willing to help with the project, though, until it comes time to eat the bread. Then she has lots of helpers, but they wonder why she doesn't bake any more bread. I am the Little Red Hen.

No one asked me to look after the rods. It was just a task that needed to be done, so I took it on. Sometimes the connections between segments had to be reinforced or cut down to stronger wood. It was a shame to shorten a rod and I only did so as a last resort, but sometimes I had to.

No one asked me to find a more vibrant orange for the floats, either. The red, in my opinion, was hard to see against the slate-coloured water. Imagine everyone's pleasure when the new neon fluorescent orange of the floats made them vibrant and easy to follow as they rode the swells.

No one asked me to tie leaders of a consistent length on an assortment of shapes and colours of teardrop hooks. Experience had taught me that in the cold, on the Rock, my numb fingers were clumsy at tying hooks. It was much better to do it at home, at the comfort of my dining room table, my hands warm and supple, the lighting good, and a selection of the proper tools within easy reach. There was no pressure, no fear of dropping small parts to be lost forever in the rocks at my feet. No one said, "No, no, Paul, you keep those pre-tied hooks. You worked hard to make them. I'm perfectly happy to tie my line myself with frozen fingers on this iceberg over here."

Don't get me wrong. I liked this role. It gave me a sense of purpose, if not importance. It made the experience richer and more meaningful for me. *I* had selected the hooks, tied the leaders, and devised a system for keeping the hooks and leaders organized and ready for immediate deployment. *I* had painted the floats and sealed the high visibility paint with lacquer. And, the night before fishing, *I* had sorted the maggots.

Someone had to do this job of sorting the living from the dead. Maggots are useful when they are wriggling. Once they reach the pupa stage and have turned black, they are of little use for fishing. Sorting maggots involves removing the unusable ones, making sure the sawdust is fresh and clean, and putting them in pill bottles so each fisherman has a ready supply.

I also learned that a few careful minutes at the end of fishing could save a lot of time at the beginning of the next trip. If the rods were stored carefully, and the line wrapped and secured, it made the walk back through the branches much easier.

"You take after your maternal grandmother's side of the family," Dad remarked once. I took that as a compliment.

There were times over the years when I was unable to go fishing with my father and brother, Dan – times when they went without the Little Red Hen. Those were difficult times for the gear. I knew the rods would come back stowed as if they had been wrapped by a band of marauding chimpanzees in hurricane force winds. There would be no order, or only the slightest semblance of order. It would be a disaster that would take several hours to unravel and make right again. I knew that maggot sawdust would be spilled in my rucksack, perhaps with one or two live maggots still milling about on the loose. On one such trip, Dad presented me sheepishly with my fibreglass rod, broken in the lower section. He explained apologetically that he'd lost his footing and had fallen on it. I forgave him and repaired the rod.

Still, sometimes it sucks to be the Little Red Hen. I have to be the big brother at the same time. Dan is seven years younger than I am. He is a party going someplace to happen. The party begins when Dan arrives. That sounds harsher than I mean it. To be fair, he *is* the life of the party. The party *does* begin when he arrives. Everything is more fun with him along. He has a quick wit and can deliver a comeback line with perfect timing. He also doesn't let me get away with anything.

Dan sure has my number. Because I am the big brother, it is his job to poke fun at me without mercy. His sole preparation for fishing is to roll out of bed and get dressed. And he often catches more fish than I do!

One time, he brought a video camera to the Rock. He always had the coolest toys. It is the only video we have of fishing on the Rock in all those years.

In the video, we are clowning for the camera. Dad is at the fire, warming his cheese sandwich on a stick. Fish are flying in and landing on stone. The Rock is glistening. We are happy and excited. It is the White Fish Festival in full swing.

Later in the video, Dad is talking to me but looking into the camera. "Dan knows how to catch them," he says.

The words burn me like a hot poker in my heart. Sure, Dan knows how to catch them, but so does the Little Red Hen. The Little Red Hen knows how to catch them, and tie leaders, and paint floats, *and* clean fish – and how to put a rod away *correctly*.

No, *The Little Red Hen* is not a story for children. It is not a recipe, either. It is not a sermon or a punchline. It is *my* story. I am the Little Red Hen. I grind wheat while the party is sound asleep.

HAND TIGHT

In "The Summer of the Family Reunion," as it shall forever be known, we convoyed to South Dakota, with a quick tour through Yellowstone National Park. Normal people might set aside a week to explore the wonders of Yellowstone. People on a time constraint should still be able to see most of the highlights in three days. The extended Rath family did it in one. We raced along the narrow, winding roads from one attraction to the next, dodging bison. We sprinted to the lookouts, snapped our pictures, then loaded back up.

The thing is, we weren't fishing or preaching. We were in normal life, which is to say, we were out of our depth. We travelled in two cars. My family in one, Kathy's in another, and our parents we shared between us. We each pulled a tent trailer. Dad often rode in our car, but we switched things up. Sometimes Mom did. We visited as we travelled to the family reunion together. The car was a mobile living room. The windscreen was a television.

Things were a little tense as we exited Yellowstone. We had waited a long time on Old Faithful, then were rushing to make it to the East Gate before it closed. I was driving on fumes. The closest gas station was outside of Yellowstone, miles and miles away.

Up to this point, our living room had been giving us a bit of trouble along the way. Every time we had stopped for gas, our home had refused to start for 30 minutes or so. Once its engine cooled down, it would fire right up and run for hours, until we stopped again for gas.

This time, we made it to Custer, South Dakota, pulled into a campground, and stopped at the registration office. Sure enough, after I registered, the living room refused to start. It was a real joker.

"I could move the trailer with *my* car," Cecil suggested.

Good idea! Well, let's just say we tried it, but the ball on his trailer hitch was the wrong size. Still, that was no problem for a man perhaps a little tired of our car's reluctance to keep moving. He deftly took the ball off my hitch, moved the trailer, then put the ball back on, hand tight.

The next morning I drove to a local garage and explained the situation. The mechanic diagnosed the problem as "vapour lock." He suggested that I could put a wooden clothespin on the metal fuel line, just before it entered the carburetor; or I could add a gallon of diesel fuel to my gas. Dad and I looked at him as if we had somehow passed into an alternate universe. How on earth would a wooden clothes pin act as a heat sink on a metal fuel line? What kind of advice were we receiving about putting diesel fuel into a gas-burning engine? I scratched my head in disbelief.

Just then, another customer walked in and basically suggested exactly the same two solutions to our problem, just in choicer words. It was like a dream that made no sense, except it was not a dream.

I had little faith in the clothespin trick and refused to put diesel in my gas tank. I had the mechanic change my fuel filter.

After the family reunion, we made our way back to Canada. Whenever we pulled out of a parking lot, the trailer hitch seemed to drag a bit. We joked that we had spent too much and were loaded down.

Here's what you need to know to understand what happened next. As I was growing up, Dad and I would watch the launches of the Apollo spacecraft. We would get up early, sit in front of the black-and-white TV, and listen to the countdown. Space exploration had captured my imagination. I was crazy about the command module, the L.E.M., and space travel. Years later, I visited Cape Canaveral and stood at the launch pad that had been used for the Apollo missions. I stood underneath a full-sized Saturn V rocket with all of its six million parts, and marvelled at the size of the rocket engines.

As we were humming north along the Interstate in The Year of the Family Reunion, I suddenly remembered watching the command module dock with the L.E.M. and pull it free in preparation for the lunar landing. In the gravity-free environment of space, everything moved in ultra-slow motion. Back in the 1960s, we had been prepared for the real thing by diagrams and simulations, and explanations about what would happen each step of the way. That's why I remembered it. I remembered it because it is burned into my soul.

So here's the thing. I was an hour from the Canadian border, on a four-lane divided highway, when I heard a thump, not much of anything really, coming from behind me. I learned later it was the safety chain failing. I looked in the rear-view mirror to see my tent trailer, like a reverse spacecraft docking procedure, pulling away from me in slow motion.

I watched as the tent trailer suddenly veered to the right and into the ditch.

"Oh," I thought, "that's good. It will just lose momentum and slow down in the ditch." This was preferable to having it crash into other traffic, of which there was lots.

No sooner had that thought formed in my mind, though, than the tongue of the tent trailer came down, like a pole vaulter setting his pole into the slot. The tent trailer rode the tongue and flipped, landing upside down on its fibreglass roof, wheels still spinning.

"Oh," I said, deadpan. "The tent trailer just hit the ditch."

Kathy and her carful were ahead of us, so they did not know we were in trouble.

I pulled over and backed along the shoulder to the crash site. The plywood table, which had once been inside the trailer, had smashed through the fibreglass roof. There was other assorted camping gear strewn about.

After assessing the situation with awe, I decided to flip the trailer over. Loaded, it probably weighed 1,600 pounds. The tongue made an excellent lever. Dad and I, along with my first wife, Laureen, lifted. Straining, we got the trailer to a 45-degree angle.

"I can't," Laureen said.

"Just do it," I replied through gritted teeth.

A final surge of adrenaline gave us just enough energy to have the tent trailer pointing straight up and down. We could not risk getting underneath it, so I made the decision to push it over.

We later learned that the ball had come off the hitch. It had only been hand-tightened, and over the thousands of miles had vibrated loose. The bolt that should have been holding it was long gone.

A Good Samaritan, who worked for the Burlington Northern Railway, had seen the incident. He had driven past because he had to attend to an urgent matter, but then returned to help. He identified the problem, said he had a ball that he thought would work, went home to get it, came back, installed it, and towed us out of the ditch.

In the meantime, a state trooper arrived. Sweat was trickling down my back in the air-conditioned cruiser as he asked me the details. He did not charge me with anything, which was fortunate. I bet he dined out on the story for years.

As we said goodbye to the Good Samaritan, I wanted to give him something for his trouble. Between us, Dad and I had about $12 U.S. A 50 would have been more like it. I offered him all the money we had, but he would not accept anything. I told him that if he ever came to visit, I would put him in front of a steak that would be too big for him to eat.

We stayed in touch for years – exchanged Christmas cards, even – and then lost track of each other. He never took me up on the steak.

Now I am paying it forward in his memory. If I see people who are in trouble, I do my best to help. If a car is parked at the side of the road in the middle of nowhere, I slow down to see if they need assistance. Often, I stop. A car might not be a fishing hole, but it is also not a living room. Life is out there, between the waves and the rocks, and it needs some care. It is, after all, only hand tight.

SMALL WORLD

Ralph had been to the Point with me many times before. We had brought his daughters once, and I had brought my sons. We had walked in together, had fished for white fish together, and had shared the fish bucket on the way back.

Along the way to the Rock was a rope, four inches in diameter, tied high on a ponderosa pine. All of the children wanted to take turns on the swing, but I was anxious to get to the Point. We let each child have a turn and promised there would be more time on our way back.

Ralph is important in my life. He is a good friend. He's the one who introduced me to the magic of composting and raised-bed gardening, and to the secret of red wigglers that eat their weight in organic material each and every day. I have focused on this commitment to the earth for 30 years. On that first day of my adventure in composting, we were in his garden and he was showing me a raised bed filled with compost, which he called "brown gold." It seemed as if the weight of the spade alone would cause it to sink into the soil. Ralph grabbed a handful of compost and formed it into a ball.

"Ideal soil," he explained, "is when you can form a ball out of it, then poke it with your finger and it falls apart."

Which it did. I was an instant convert. He gave me a milk jug full of red wrigglers, which he was setting himself up to market as "Kompost Kings."

"They will provide me with fame and fortune," he said.

I told him my grandfather had farmed in southern Alberta, right up against the U.S. border. He replied that his grandfather had farmed in southern Alberta, right up against the U.S. border. I told him that my father had attended a one-room schoolhouse in Kimball. He replied that his mother had attended a one-room schoolhouse in

Kimball. Comparing the age of my father and the age of his mother, we surmised that our parents not only went to the same one-room schoolhouse, but were there at approximately the same time and undoubtedly knew each other. We stared at each other in disbelief. How had we not known this about each other? We had worked together, hunted together, and had gone to the range together. We had shot handguns into a box of telephone books to see how much further a .357 magnum penetrated compared to a .38 Special. We were good friends. It never occurred to us that our parents had history together. After checking with our parents, we determined that Ralph's mother was in the same grade as my uncle George, and knew my father, who was a few years younger. It really *is* a small, small world.

"My father said he threw a handful of .22 cartridges into the wood stove that heated the schoolhouse, before taking his seat, and waited for the pop-pop-pop when the cartridges exploded," I told Ralph.

Ralph laughed.

"He skied down the slopes at Kimball, too," I said. "His skis were just boards he tied onto his feet."

"What did he use for poles?" Ralph asked.

"He slid down the slope without poles," I answered. We laughed.

I met Ralph while I was selling life insurance. We both endured that hardship together. Ralph had left a position with the soul-sucking federal government to seek his fortune with his own financial services franchise. We both had had fancy business cards printed. We both agree now that the only good thing to come out of that difficult time in our lives was our friendship, which has lasted 30 years.

One day when just Ralph and I were at the Rock, I set him up with the primary spot, where my father usually fished. I took my regular spot, the secondary spot, and caught fish after fish, while Ralph caught only one or two. He wanted to trade places with me, and I readily agreed.

In the primary spot, I caught fish after fish. Ralph was frustrated and did not understand. I had him move back into the primary spot again, leaned my rod against the rocks behind us and stood at his elbow. I told him to focus on the float. I told him when he was fishing dead water and needed to recast.

"Just by looking at your float," I said, "I can tell that the leader is tangled on the main line."

"How do you know that?" he asked.

I didn't know how I knew, I just knew. When his float twisted in the water, I told him to get ready, that a fish was playing ever so softly with his hook, and to expect a bite. The stick lifted, Ralph pulled, and in an instant the fish was landed and in the pail. I continued to stand at his elbow as he began to focus on the signs independently and to catch fish on his own. He was beginning to speak float language.

"Paul Rath, fishing consultant," he said.

I laughed and took up my rod again. It was only later, as I thought through the experience of standing at his elbow and interpreting float language for him, that I realized that I knew how to catch white fish like I knew my own name. I have been fishing white fish for nearly 50 years. I had put in the time and had learned the craft. I had become a master, in spite of myself.

I'll forego the business card, though.

FALLING IN

In all the years that I took the long walk to the Point and stood like a shivering goat on the icy rocks, teetering precariously above the cold water, I never fell in. Not once. That is not to say that I didn't often lose my balance and lurch drunkenly, flapping my arms and doing whatever it took to regain my balance to *keep* from falling in. I did that plenty. That is also not to say that I didn't ever go home wet. I often got soaked. Sometimes I was soaked from my thighs down by the waves that crashed against the rocks and that sprayed me or washed over my boots and filled them with icy water.

My sons were not as fortunate as I was about falling in. Both of them ended up in the lake. My oldest son, Jonathan, fell in more than once.

All a fisherman needs to know is that a child, wet to the skin in freezing weather, becomes a critical situation. Fishing ceases.

First, the child has to be rescued from the water, then immediately stripped of wet clothing. In my case, if I was lucky, they were not soaked to the skin. On those lucky days, I could just remove the wet layers, dress them with dry clothing I was wearing, and continue fishing.

If they *were* soaked to the skin, fishing was over for the day. The wet clothing had to be removed, some of my dry layers had to be shared, and we had to pack up and head to the car like a troop of sad clowns to face their mother's disapproval.

What was I doing that my children were unattended to the extent that they could fall in, you might ask? Laureen, sure did, so go ahead. My answer is the same as ever; I was fishing. And because you've read this far in this book, you know what that means; I was focusing on my float.

I tried to teach my sons to fish, and to some extent succeeded. Once, when we were fishing salmon on the Skeena – that great river of the

North – I told my younger son, Aaron, that its water held the fish of his dreams.

"Dad," he said. "I don't dream about fish."

It broke my heart.

Jonathan was good with fishing as long as the fish were biting, but when the fishing was slow he needed other things to stimulate him.

Dad and I discouraged him from throwing rocks into the lake. Behind us, there was a little bush area he could explore. That seemed harmless enough.

It wasn't. It made me drop my guard. Sometimes, as I talked to Dad, and focused on my float, I was not paying as much attention to my children as I should have. In this particular instance, the next thing I knew neither of them was in the bush and one of them had fallen into the lake. Immediate action had to be taken to keep him from becoming hypothermic. Dad, bless him, kept on fishing.

One time, Aaron fell in and soaked everything but his undershorts. I quickly stripped him down and my turtleneck sweater became his new pants. My outer sweater replaced his coat.

When the boys' boots were wet, I put plastic bags over their feet, then inserted their feet back into the wet boots. Dad reluctantly pulled in his last fish and, while the boys waited, shivering, I grabbed Dad's rod and packed it up before he could cast out again, or before he could step on it. Then we were off.

The boys squished water all the way back to the car. Dad didn't say a thing. But that said more than words ever could. The rhythmic squish, squish was my music now, and the boys and I had to face it alone, together.

FISHING PARTNER

No one likes to be stood up. I had arranged a trip to the Rock with Dan. I was going to pick him up at his apartment. With the drive, the walk to the Rock along the shore, and my desire to be there rigged and ready for first light, we agreed that I'd pick him up at 5 a.m.

I never sleep well the night before a fishing trip. There's just too much to do. I get the gear ready to grab and go, sort the maggots, freshen their sawdust if necessary, get out the thermos, and put everything in order so my morning will go smoothly. I go to bed early, set a couple of alarms, but then I am often too keyed up to sleep. When I do doze off, I seem to wake up every hour, as if my internal alarm clock, like an elevator that has had the buttons pressed to stop on every floor, wakes me up like clockwork in one-hour increments. It is exhausting.

This time, I arrived at Dan's apartment on time. He was not ready.

"Come up," he said. He buzzed me in.

I was annoyed that he wasn't ready, but when I entered his apartment I saw at once that not only was he not ready, he had not yet been to bed. He and his roommate had spent the night drinking and were in more of a party mood than a fishing mood.

I was *not* the life of this party. I was dressed in layers, ready for the November wind, but it wasn't my long johns that made me hot in his apartment. I got angry and then guilted the two of them to get ready and come with me.

"Dress warmly," I snapped, "and in layers."

I didn't police their choices, so it was only when we were on the Rock that I noticed that the roommate had dress shoes on, which were not only slippery on the rocks but had zero thermal heating value. In my world, you don't mess with a precious white fish day like that.

Then I noticed that neither of them was dressed appropriately. Also, the effects of the alcohol were wearing off, and the lack of sleep was kicking in. Dan's stick was not standing up. Dan's float was not lying flat on the water. Dan's float was in fact a foot under the surface. A fish had taken the hook and was trying to swim away with it.

"Go, Dan," I said impatiently, probably missing a bite of my own in the process. He jerked up on his rod, but by then the fish had cleaned all the maggots off and spit out the hook.

I said, "Go, Dan," quite often on that frosty morning, until they were both not fishing but sitting on the Rock, nearly asleep. Finally, I took pity on them and called it a day.

We have told that story over the years. It has become part of our culture. The fish are long eaten, the roommate long since moved away, and the details are not as crisp as they once were, but I still say "Go, Dan," and now that he's sobered up he laughs, because what else do you do when you know exactly what that means.

VIBRATOR

Dad and I were fishing on the Rock, once again able to talk about anything, joke with each other, and even trade insights.

"You are paid to be good," I said.

Without taking his eyes off his float, he said, "A layman is good for nothing."

At that I took my eye off my float and looked at him carefully. He just kept fishing.

Soon we were talking about how challenging my oldest son was, and about how I disagreed with Laureen, the mother of my children, about how to deal with him. He answered by listening.

So imagine my shock as I stood on the rock, balanced precariously above the cold waters of Okanagan Lake in November, when my father said to me, "Your mother and I bought a vibrator."

I sputtered, teetered, nearly lost my balance, fought to regain both my balance and my composure, all while still hanging on to my rod and keeping an eye on my float.

"Oh," was all I could manage, my mind racing in 60 directions, none of them good. But I *did* stay on the rock and did *not* fall into the cold water.

Nothing was off limits between us, but really? A vibrator? I was not sure I wanted to have this conversation with my father.

I just waited, said nothing, focused on my float, and prayed for a fish to take my mind off the situation I had found myself in.

"The doctor said it would help my back," he explained.

I let out a huge sigh of relief. We were not actually having *that* conversation after all.

I found out that he had paid about $500 for it, which was a small fortune. It was German-made and very powerful. I have it now and, 20 years after his death, it still works fine and is good for my back.

After a while, I told him that a *vibrator* was very different than a *massager*. We laughed about that, when I explained to him what a vibrator was.

And, yeah, he took his eye off his float.

CENTENNIAL PROJECT

We were out on the Rock one frosty November morning. We didn't even see the eagle, but he was obviously watching us. The fish weren't biting, but as if in compensation the waves were coming in like music and my float was rising up over them with the grace of a pair of hands on a church organ.

"Do you remember the Centennial Project?" I asked.

"Sure," Dad replied. "The piano."

Yes, the piano. In 1967, Canada marked 100 years of Confederation. The country celebrated with special coins designed by the renowned artist Alex Colville. His iconic images of Canadian wildlife were struck in pure silver. There was also a series of new stamps, and a museum train that travelled from coast to coast, with exhibits of Canada's history.

I have a set of the coins, and the stamps, and I even have a stamp box with the Centennial stamps on the lid, which holds my stamps and the multitude of address labels various charities send me. Somehow, they all know where I live. I'm not paranoid or anything, but I think they talk to each other.

Last summer, Canada celebrated 150 years of Confederation. I bought a couple of coin sets, one re-issuing the iconic Colville animals with the new dates on them, and a special-circulation coin set. I also planted some *Canada 150* tulips. They were red and white. I was lucky enough to have them bloom on Canada Day.

That quiet pleasure paled beside the joy of 1967, when I was ten years old and travelled to Beaverlodge, Alberta, to tour the Centennial train. It had the first four notes of *O Canada* as its whistle. I was in love.

Beaverlodge was our doorway to the world. It had the local hospital. It was where I learned to swim, where Dan was born, where my father bought his only brand new car, and where they took me the morning I had an appendicitis attack and my leg seemed stitched to my stomach and I had a hard time putting my pants on.

My parents decided that since the country was celebrating 100 years of past achievements, it was a good time for us as a family to set some goals ourselves. They bought a piano and enrolled all of us children in piano lessons.

That year, my father drove us to Beaverlodge weekly. My sisters and I waited our turn to sit on the piano bench and receive our lesson. Dan wasn't yet born. He had to wait longer for this fun.

While I was waiting in the piano teacher's living room, I explored the mysterious world of sexuality in the volumes of the *World Book Encyclopedia*. We did not have a set of encyclopedias at home. What I learned about the mysteries of the female human body, human procreation, and sexually transmitted diseases was all in the encyclopedia – if you knew where to look. I learned quickly that if you knew one word, at the end of the article were ten words you didn't know, and you could check those out, too. I learned more than my ten-year-old self should have. As a result, I didn't mind going to piano lessons.

The piano lessons themselves were a disaster. It's not that I am not musical. I can read music in the waves, for instance. I can even play the piano – by ear. However, I never developed the discipline to look at notes and relate them to the keys. If they had been a neon-coloured float, sure, but they weren't.

After a year or so, the piano teacher met with my father and asked him not to bring me to practice my piano lessons at her house anymore. It was just as well, as by that time most of my research was complete.

It was the same years later, when I took guitar in Grade 11. The final exam was playing a classical song called "Larghetto." I played by ear. If our teacher had asked me to start in the middle, I would have been sunk. I had memorized the piece and played the entire song without knowing how to read a note of music.

Actually, that is not true. I can pick out middle C on the notation. It's my float.

My teacher played in some band on the weekends and once called one of my classmates a boor for coming in late with an attitude. The student did not know what a boor was, so he was sent to the library to look up the word and report back. Books and music lessons have always had a close connection in my world.

My sisters are both very musical. Kathy sings in two choirs and has even directed the choir from time to time. Her daughter is a school music teacher. My other sister, Rose, has taught piano lessons for years. Both play the guitar and various other instruments. Rose collects musical instruments from around the world. Kathy plays trumpet, Rose the clarinet, *and* they both can read music. Amazing.

Dad was like that. He played guitar and yodelled. He also played an instrument called a melodica, which combined woodwind and keyboard technology. He could also squeeze out some tunes on the accordion. One day he came home with an apparatus made of stainless steel that would hold a mouth organ to his lips while he strummed his guitar. Something Neil Young would do. Dad was cool. He loved to play the guitar and yodel at both church and family functions. I don't know if Neil Young has experienced such heights, too. I hope so, for his sake.

After the leprosy came back, Dad and I were visiting a specialist in Vancouver.

"Will I be able to play the guitar again?" Dad asked.

"No," the specialist answered.

"Not ever?" Dad asked, crestfallen.

"Not ever," the doctor said adamantly.

As we were walking back to the car, I could tell Dad was shell-shocked by the news.

"I can't believe what the doctor said," he told me.

"Doctors don't know everything," I said. "He just gave an opinion – an educated opinion, but just an opinion nonetheless."

"Do *you* think I will be able to play the guitar again?" he asked me.

"I'm not a doctor," I said, "but people can do amazing things. He doesn't know the future. Only God knows that. I think you can do pretty much anything you set your mind to. God is still in charge."

He seemed comforted by that and *did* regain enough feeling in his fingers to play and yodel for many years after the visit with the doctor, even though he did become terrible at tying teardrop hooks to frozen fishing line.

The piano we bought for our Centennial Project was brand new. A year or so after we had bought it, though, we began to notice that the notes around middle C (see it wasn't a total waste) sounded funny when you hit them.

We opened the lid and found a mouse nest built inside the piano, filled with six pink-skinned baby mice. My parents were shopping in Grande Prairie, Alberta, when we made this discovery. We were home alone.

The net result was that the mother mouse made her escape, but her progeny wound up carefully placed in the stylish glass bowl that adorned our coffee table. We planned to keep them as pets.

We were excited to show our parents our find and to explain that we had "fixed" the piano. We presented them with the mice in the ornamental bowl.

"Can we keep them as pets?" I asked, as the designated sibling lightning rod.

"No," Dad said. "You cannot keep them as pets."

I can't remember what my mother said, but it doesn't matter. We had Dad's attention. We persisted, whining and asking again. Now that I had broken the ground, we *all* asked, just like a squirming bundle of little pink rodents.

I guess we weren't as cute as we thought, because he suddenly grabbed the bowl from us and took it outside to the gravel driveway, grabbed a stick as he was passing out the door, dumped the wriggling contents on the rocks, and then smashed the mice with the stick. The answer was no.

Kathy and Rose were mortified. I was in awe. None of us had known my father hated mice that much or could even act that way. Years later my sisters told me it was one of the most traumatic experiences of their childhood.

I was saddened that it had been so traumatic. For me, it was an example of my father's single-minded practicality.

The piano ended up with Dan. Kathy and Rose already had pianos of their own. I got the boat.

"Right, the piano," I answered that November morning when we were discussing our Centennial Project. "You know, I never learned to read music," I said.

"Me neither," Dad replied. "Me neither."

Just then, the eagle appeared. He had seen one of the fish we threw back and glided off from the mountainside without a sound. He swung his talons down and plucked the fish from the surface of the water and again soundlessly lifted back to his lookout.

Dad and I glanced at each other, surprised and awed by the majestic display. A single tuft of eagle down, the only evidence of the event, hovered in the air above us, then slowly drifted to the west.

ANGINA

My father was a large man. So am I. So is Dan. There is some question about who was bigger – my father, Dan, or me. Dan and I often trade places. Although I am seven years older, I am not always the big brother. It is especially aggravating to him if I call him "big brother," so I do it as often as I can. Fortunately for him, he has recently lost 40 pounds, so currently the title of Largest Rath is between my father and me.

My father knew how to work a buffet table. I have no such excuse. He never had more than two or three things on his napkin, but he always had two or three things on his napkin. In his line of work, food was always available. At every wedding, funeral, or congregational meeting, some ladies would bring what he called "goodies." He thought they were *very* good.

He liked food of any kind and was partial to corn on the cob, especially if roasted on a screen over an open fire. He liked his steak well done, which to me was like eating charcoal right out of the bag. I tried for years to convert him to medium rare, but my teasing was fruitless. Together, we often raided the freezer where my mother stored cookies and squares for special occasions: Christmas, Easter, church functions, birthdays, etc. To this day, I prefer cookies and squares frozen or partially frozen. When my mother complained about her stores being raided, I told her that at least we were eating them, and not burying them in the backyard like Elly May's family did to her cookies on *The Beverly Hillbillies*.

My father eventually developed angina because the arteries around his heart were so lined with "goodies" that they failed to provide his big heart with an adequate blood supply. That's why years later he died in his sleep. He just lay down, said his prayers, and drifted off. If I could choose a way to go, that would be high on my list.

His death took us all by surprise. For one thing, he was only 69 and did not appear ill at all. It was like being sucker-punched in the head. One minute you are sitting there, and the next you are down on the floor, dazed and confused, wondering what happened. I know what happened. He was obese. It seems to be a family hazard.

It took me a long time to be able to talk about his death coherently. I was at work when the call came. My sister Kathy and brother-in-law Cecil were on the phone and asking me to sit down. My mother was in the hospital at the time. My mind raced ahead. Mom was gone. She had not come through the surgery ... but it was not Mom who was gone. It was Dad.

I could not believe it. "Dad?" I asked in disbelief.

I was sure they were confused. Mom was the one in hospital. She was in poor health and at risk for not coming out of the surgery. Surely, they meant Mom.

They meant Dad. My fishing buddy. My pastor. My dad.

We were busy at the border that night. Traffic had been waiting on me for a few minutes, when I stumbled back to clear a car.

"Coffee break?" the traveller asked in sarcastic annoyance.

"No," I said deadpan, still in shock, my voice flat. "I just found out my dad died."

I don't remember his response.

But that was years after the morning in question. On this morning, Dad and I were heading to the Rock. I was carrying the rods under one arm, switching to the other when it grew tired, and had a rucksack from my father-in-law's army days slung over one shoulder. It held hooks, line, spare floats, and gear. I was excited and walking fast. Dad was carrying the fish pail. It held our lunch. Fishing works up an appetite.

The trail to the first cabin was broad and flat. Just before the first cabin, some wiseacre had planted a highway speed sign in a 45-gallon drum to the right of the trail. We joked about this speed limit because we were often in a hurry to get fishing. We always stopped at the sign with first timers and urged them to keep their speed down.

"The problem of people going too fast is so bad," I told them, "a sign had been posted on this trail. Keep it down."

This time we hurried past. We almost broke the limit. I had skirted the first cabin and was closing in on the second when I noticed Dad was not behind me. There were no footfalls behind me and no crunch of crisp dry leaves beneath his feet. I was alone. I went back.

I found him leaning against the wall of the first cabin, straining to catch his breath. He was clutching at his chest, his face openly showing the pain he was experiencing. We debated briefly if he was well enough to continue. I thought we should head back. He said he would be okay if he could just catch his breath. We paused while he caught his breath and were able to carry on. I slowed the pace after that.

Since then, I've often thought about what I would have done if Dad had had a heart attack out on the Rock that day. He was too heavy to carry. As I figured it many times, I basically had two choices: either leave him and race back down the trail to one of the houses above the beach and hope someone was home, or push him into the lake and float him back to the car. The second option reminded me of a certain four-point buck.

Neither scenario seemed promising. We were literally risking our lives.

I should have known better. At 90, my grandfather Jacob had died of a heart attack. When the pains first started, it was 3 a.m. and he refused to seek help. He lay in pain for several hours, while his heart was damaged, until around 6 a.m. when my grandmother, Jacob's third wife, convinced him to seek help. They called me, and I took him to the hospital emergency department.

As he lay on the bed, he was given medication. An attending doctor asked if it was helping and he replied, "Like smoke to the dead."

The doctor did not understand the colourful way my grandfather spoke. I translated. "He says it is not helping at all," I said.

He was later admitted to the hospital. After almost a week, he had improved enough that he was cleared to be released. He was up shaving, getting ready to come home and singing in his deep bass voice when the second and final heart attack came.

Dad and I enjoyed our time on the Rock the morning of his angina attack. Perhaps we enjoyed it more than usual and were focusing extra hard on our floats because the reality of my father clutching his chest in discomfort from just walking down the trail reminded us how fleeting our time is on this earth. It is one thing to stand on the rocks talking about life and death and everything in between. It is quite another to be confronted with the stark reality that we all owe a death, and that payment can come due at any moment. Each fish we caught, after all, had the potential to be our last.

All his life, my father directed people to the spiritual path and then let them take the lead from there. He had a sense of urgency to show people "the Way." He was just a pilgrim, pointing people to the path, realizing that this was not his home. That's not to say he didn't enjoy the beauty of God's world around him. He was well-travelled and had seen many of the Earth's wonders. He also marvelled at the mystery of how white fish came to be at the Point for a few short weeks each November, without fail.

Now, though, he has taken the lead. It is comforting to know that he has gone ahead and is waiting for me, leaning against the pearly gates, probably with fishing gear in his hand. As I approach 63, my own mortality stares at me. Dad died at 69. Do I have six years left? Less? More?

At least he has gone ahead, kicking the stones off the path, breaking off branches, and is there, waiting. I want to see him again, but I am not in a rush. I still have a lot of fishing to do.

DEAD WRONG

My father dispensed good counsel and advice at all times, in keeping with our family name Rath, which means just that: advice.

Unlike me, in his entire life my father was only ever wrong about two things. He once told me that "life begins when the children leave home and the dog dies." He was wrong, dead wrong, on both counts. Perhaps he was only joking. Perhaps he said it for effect. Sometimes he liked to say outrageous things just to see if I was paying attention.

On this occasion, I was. It was a cold November morning. My youngest son, Aaron, was leaving home for the second time. The raw drizzle matched my mood. I helped him load his car but became alarmed once he had it started. The smell of raw gas permeated the rain and nearly overwhelmed me. A quick check under the hood revealed that his carburetor was leaking gas onto the engine block, a great place to burst into flame. I felt like a failure when I was unable to convince him to stay one more day to have it repaired. He was off to seek his fortune in the oil patch. I felt like I was sending him to a fiery death instead of out to conquer the world. I tightened things as best as I could, hugged him, and wished him Godspeed.

That was a difficult day, as were the ones that followed. Even now, a dozen years later, I still feel a void and a sense of loss, though he is married and has a son of his own. Life did *not* begin for me that day, as my father had predicted. Quite the opposite. Part of it seemed to end. I wondered if I had done enough and had sufficiently prepared my son for life on his own. My mistakes, which were many, leaned against the corner of the house, talking and joking loudly amongst themselves, sneering in my direction. They blatantly accused me, laughing at my expense, knowing I had no defence because I was out of time: no more time to do things again, to make better decisions, to focus on the right priorities.

My father's cute saying made no sense. When he settled my grandfather's estate, the money was to be divided equally between three siblings. My aunt Freda lived in the United States. My father felt that he should top up her share so that each sibling received the same dollar amount. Since the U.S. dollar was worth more than the Canadian one, she seemed to be getting less. Dad's arithmetic showed him that for every $1,000 Canadian, she was only getting getting $750 American. He couldn't stand for that, so out of his own pocket he threw in the difference in exchange.

That's the way he was. So why did he think getting rid of children was life itself? "Old monkeys don't jump on rotten limbs," he told me once, giving me notice that he had some experience. He had a rhyme in German that also worked in English. "A man convinced against his will, is of the same opinion still." Another: "Buy the best quality you can afford. Don't go crazy, but quality always pays its way." That was good advice, and has served me well. But about life beginning when the children leave home and the dog dies – he was off the mark.

Maybe he never bonded with a dog. It is said that a dog is the only creature that will love you more than you love yourself. Maybe that's it. He certainly grew up with dogs on the farm, but they were not pets. They were outside dogs that looked after things on the farm, announced the arrival of visitors, chased off predators, and performed other work functions. I doubt that they ever warmed my father's feet on his bed, or woke him in the morning by licking his face. I doubt that they ever looked at him with such innocent longing and trust that thinking about the purity of it breaks your heart.

I remember one of the farm dogs got into a porcupine. My father and grandfather removed the quills from his mouth. They sat with the dog in the garage, pulling the quills out with pliers. There was no money for a visit to the vet's office. It was the way things were. The dog didn't lick my father's face in thanks.

Moose was a Maltese Shih Tzu. He was a little white dog who nuzzled his way into my heart, and chose a beautiful day to say goodbye. It was far too soon. We had only had him in our lives for ten years.

Up on the pass, the blue sky and the bright sunshine made the snowcapped mountain peaks stand out with fearsome beauty. The sun told us to "look here." I was distracted by the beauty all around me, momentarily forgetting that Moose was still panting, obviously in distress, and could not find a comfortable position in which to sleep. The vet was hours away, and the visit to the vet was likely to be Moose's last. As I glanced at the mountain peaks, I momentarily forgot why we were bundled in the car and heading to town.

Moose had developed a cough in the summer. We took him in and they gave him something for inflammation. They said he might have a foxtail caught in his throat. The cough persisted. Another visit and an x-ray revealed congestive heart failure. They said we could have a week, or a year.

He was patient with us as we tried to keep him eating, when for no good reason he would boycott the food that he had been eating for weeks. Another visit to the vet and an ultrasound gave us the sad news that his heart was enlarged, that he had an infection in his tooth, and a special diet would likely extend his life. We made dog food ourselves, using ground turkey, vegetables, and rice. He was on a plethora of medications. We were given week after precious week.

He would get excited and then faint because there was not enough blood going to his brain. It was as if someone had turned his switch off. He would hit the floor with a thump and usually evacuate his bladder. A few seconds later he would be awake and acting as if nothing had happened.

He was normal otherwise.

It was a Monday morning in early January. He was outside and suddenly passed out. This time he stiffened and cried out in pain as a seizure rocked through him. It was a mournful sound of pain and bewilderment. It shook me and continued to concern me when he could not catch his breath.

On the way to the vet, he was able to sleep for a while, and I wondered if maybe it would be okay. Later, he sat up, stretching his neck, panting, trying to find a position of comfort, and I knew that things would not be okay.

I carried him into the examination room while they explained the procedure to me and I signed the paperwork. I just wanted them to make his suffering stop. I kept saying that he was a "good boy" and I hoped he did not sense the betrayal in my eyes that I felt in my heart as they gave him some sedation to take the edge off of the rest of the procedure.

I was not there when my father died, did not hold his hand or see the light in his eyes fade. He passed in his sleep. My father was used to seeing people die. He gave comfort where he could, acknowledged and shared their pain, and sent them off to the next life.

I kept telling Moose that he was a "good boy." As the sedative kicked in, he was drifting away and did not care about the bare patch they shaved on his leg to expose the vein. I wanted to keep him with me but knew in my heart that his laboured breathing signalled that it was time for me to do the unselfish thing and let him go. He was counting on me to do the right thing, even as I sat there second guessing myself.

He jerked once when the poison hit his veins. Perhaps it felt like fire consuming him. Before he could register any alarm, the rapid breathing stopped. He was limp in my arms. I remember thinking that it was not exactly like going to sleep.

I held him to the end, told him again that he was a "good boy," and said a prayer of thanks to God for allowing this gentle heart into our lives. Then laid him on the exam table, numb with grief and guilt.

My father was a wise and learned man. He used stories to guide us with information he thought we would need. I have adopted most of his advice and have even passed it on to my own sons. The one about life beginning when the children leave home and the dog dying, I will not share.

Perhaps my father meant "eternal life" begins "when the children leave home ..."? Maybe he was tired of pulling out the quills I've always had a gift for sticking myself with?

I don't know. My father died in September. To put that into perspective, it was two-and-a-half months before white fish season. You never know when your last visit to the Rock might be.

In the week before his death, I watched with horror and fascination the never-ending news coverage of Lady Diana's deadly car crash. Hour after hour, the coverage continued. It was the news machine at its most garish and bizarre, but I couldn't look away. I was horrified yet mesmerized at the same time. I remember thinking that one day it would be our turn to ride in the black limousines. They would come for us.

Until then, we had been fairly unscathed by death. Sure, people I knew had died. There was Terry in Grade 4, who had liver disease. He had an eraser made of some gel-like material. I asked to see it and stuck a fingernail into it, taking a chunk out of it. He noticed the gouge and asked for my eraser, which he took a bite out of, chewed up, and then spat in my face. I thought about that after he died, his spit with bits of eraser on my face, and I wondered if I would catch whatever had killed him.

My maternal grandmother, Fanny Lethal, died when I was quite young. She was old and sick when I knew her. Only my mother went to the funeral because it was so far away.

My paternal grandmother, Mary, died one Christmas Eve. We went to that funeral. I tried to support Dad by standing at his side. My grandmother looked rather stoic in her coffin. Her mouth was stubbornly closed, as if she was preventing herself from revealing some great secret that was on the tip of her tongue.

She had lived a hard life. She had fled her home for Canada, with little but the clothes on her back. She lost two infant children and raised three. Her lips, however, had been the soft texture of eyelids whenever she had kissed me. She had loved mandarin oranges and had known how to make a feast out of flour and water. When company arrived, the contents of the fridge were always piled onto the table. She never accepted my mother, though, mostly because she was not German, and still seemed to disapprove from her final resting place.

When I was three or so, I attended a funeral in Brazil. I remember the woman's bare feet, where she was laid out. I was too small to see much of anything else. She lay on a table, and her old bare feet looked cold and worn. I had nightmares after that. About feet.

Dan and Kathy and Rose and I used to watch funerals from the parsonage. One day we watched the funeral of Cookie Grandma, an elderly woman my father used to minister to. Sometimes he had taken my younger brother along. She had given him cookies. One could do worse than go to visit Cookie Grandma.

We watched her funeral from the windows of our TV room, which looked out over the church and parking lot. The cemetery, south of the church, was just visible from our vantage point. Kathy and Rose and I told Dan that his cookie grandma was in the box, and that she was to be buried in the cemetery.

That was, perhaps, too abrupt. We had a lot of explaining to do when my mother returned from the funeral to find Dan in a frenzy of panic.

"Call Batman," he told my mother solemnly. "They have Cookie Grandma in a suitcase, and they are going to put her in the ground and cover her up."

Batman was not called. Dad and I had words. The family parish was not always the easiest one.

Now death was close and personal. Just as you never know when your last trip to the Rock will be, you don't know the last time you will speak to someone, or what your last words will be. The last time I spoke to my father, I was angry with him on the phone. My mother was in the hospital recovering from knee surgery. As we talked, making plans to visit her, my father asked me about attending church.

"That's not in my plan," I said.

"Church is important," he said to me, in an admonishing way.

Hearing those words made me angry. I knew church was important. I was a grown man, not a child.

Those were his last words to me on this earth, and all because I was angry and thought I would punish him by not stopping by after I had seen my mother. That would teach him.

My mother told me later that he waited for me all day, looking out the window, staring at the door of the hospital room, and that later in the day he went home, crushed.

My excuse to myself was that I was running late and had to get back home because I had to work the next day. That night, my father lay down to sleep and didn't wake up.

I felt like a stupid, petulant child, and debated with myself about whether I should or should not go to the Rock that first November after he died. I changed my mind a hundred times. How could I go without him? How could I not go? I would certainly miss him, in that place more than any other. I would go. I would not go. *Perhaps I should punish myself for my actions by not going:* a self-imposed penance. I went.

It was a clear day and I was alone. Fishing was slow. I caught a few fish. There was no wind. There was too much light. I perched on a rock, and watched my float, daydreaming about my father.

Suddenly I saw movement in the periphery of my vision. I looked over to see bright yellow leaves gather together from the ground, then slowly lift and swirl in a lazy circle up to the height of the trees, and then beyond.

There was no wind. There was no sound, just these swirling yellow leaves dancing upwards.

I had never seen anything like this at the Rock before, and I have never seen anything like it anywhere since. I watched as the leaves swirled upwards, then scattered and fell back to earth.

Was it a message from my father? Was it my grief seeing something more than a thermal cell forming and lifting leaves upwards? Had my father come to the Rock one last time? Was he telling me it was okay? That he was okay? That he had forgiven me for being a jack-ass? I don't believe in ghosts, or signs like that, and that is why this was so difficult, because it sure looked like one.

Houdini, the escape artist, magician, and showman, was said to have had an interest in the afterlife. He allegedly pre-arranged a password with his wife to substantiate his identity after he was dead. It was to be proof that it was possible to make contact from the other side. The password was never used.

My father and I had no such code or password that we could use to pierce the veil from one side to the other and send a message through.

Some say that when you die, that's it. There is nothing more. It's just blackness.

I don't accept that. A thinking man can't. It doesn't take much ex-amination of the physical world to see that there is an architect of the universe. To accept that all this happened by chance is so preposterous it is almost laughable. To think that white fish could have evolved from a chemical soup over millions of years was such a stretch. How did the fish know when it was time to seek out the rocky shores to spawn? I have taken many fish apart. They are complicated. Swim bladders, gills, teeth, or no teeth, teeth on the tongue or on the gill rakers.

What amazes me is the humour of the architect. God makes the rules, then freely breaks them. Mammals give birth to live young, ex-cept for the monotremes who lay eggs. Giraffes have the same number of neck vertebrae as humans. In the pocket desert near Osoyoos, there is a symbiotic relationship between the desert pocket gopher and the rabbit bush. In the desert, water is a precious commodity. A rabbit bush grows slowly. One that is 100 years old would be the size of your coffee table. When it matures, it drops seeds, which are too big to be carried by the wind but are collected as food by the pocket gopher, who takes them away and stores them in his burrows. In the coolness of the bur-row, the seeds absorb the moisture of the pocket gopher's breath and plump up. The pocket gopher drinks no water. His only water source is the seeds which give him back his recycled breath. However, the pocket gopher forgets some of his rabbit bush seed stashes, which sprout to form new rabbit bushes. Clearly there is an architect of the universe. Clearly there is more to reality than just this physical realm we inhabit.

I told no one about the swirling leaves at the Point. I could not explain or understand what I had witnessed, and who would have believed me, anyway? It was a phenomenon. That's it. An unexplained phenomenon. That's what I keep telling myself. Just between me and my Dad, though, with white fish as my witnesses, I'd like to believe it was something more.

WHEN THE STUDENT IS READY, THE TEACHER WILL APPEAR

As I reflect back on standing on the Rock, focusing on my float (or trying to) and talking about life with my father (or trying to), I am coming to realize that perhaps I was not ready to receive his lessons. That's my fault, not his. Not only was he a patient teacher, he demonstrated by his actions the lessons he was trying to teach me. He also pointed to scripture. What more could you want?

I was also not ready when my grandfather had a conversation with me about training oxen. I didn't understand that he was passing me his legacy. We were sitting together at his kitchen table. I was watching him glide the blade of the knife he was sharpening against his knife stone with all the skill and experience of his 90 years, just as his father and his father's father had done before him.

The knife sang softly as it was honed. I thought about my own helplessness with knifes – how I am held captive in my kitchen by knives that are dull – and about my frustration and lack of success in sharpening them. We won't even talk about a certain folding knife.

"To train a team of oxen," my grandfather said in a tone of authority, as if I had asked a question, as if he had to communicate this one lesson to me above the soft and rhythmic sounds the knife was making against the stone, ... "To train a team of oxen, first get them used to a yoke."

I was stuck on oxen. Why oxen? Where would I get oxen? Why would I *have* oxen? How would I *keep* oxen? What would I *feed* oxen?

I was also suddenly remembering the night in Brazil when the whole Rath family was on its way home from one of the churches my father had started. "Stations," he called them. They were simple affairs that took place in people's houses.

That night we were caught in a huge rainstorm and the red dirt of the road turned into a greasy impassible mire. We found ourselves in the middle of nowhere, in a ditch. Stuck. We waited out the night with the rain drumming on the roof of the '36 Chev. Sheet lightning brightened the sky around us. My youngest sister, Kathy, was a baby. It was a sleepless night.

The next morning my father set out for help. I told my mother, "Papa come," a thousand times, more to reassure myself than her.

It worked! After what seemed like ages, my father appeared with a farmer and a yoke of oxen. I was beside myself with joy.

The farmer hooked the oxen to the car and these strong animals pulled us out of the ditch and onto the road as if we were made of feathers.

"After that," my grandfather continued, snapping me back to his present, "hitch on a little log, and let them *pull-l-l-l*." He spoke the word pull with his deep bass voice and gave emphasis to the "l" as if it would help me understand the concept.

"After a while," he added, "hitch them to an empty wagon, then a heavier one, and so on."

I was getting the idea that training a team of oxen was a long and arduous process.

"One good team of oxen," he told me in all earnestness, as if this information was vital to my survival, "will out-pull six horses."

I smiled and nodded, as if understanding, as if I was storing this data for future use, when actually, I didn't hear a thing he meant. I was just watching him sharpen the knives, daydreaming about a traumatic night in Brazil and wishing he would teach me knife sharpening.

I did, however, write the story down in the form of a poem, and showed it to my family. It was the knife sharpening I thought I had captured. The poem takes place in the spring of the year he died. My grandfather and I are sitting at his kitchen table, drinking buttermilk while he sharpens his knives. His garden is patiently awaiting him: a hoe leaning in a corner by the back step, its blade polished silver by the dark earth, his hat perched on the back of his chair. The patches on his faded blue coveralls seem as out of place as his youthful clear blue eyes seem in his lined face. It was a nice poem, but I had cast his gems away, carelessly, like a foolish character in a Russian fairytale. The student had not been ready. I had missed the point yet had faithfully copied his words into the poem. That was good, although the poem ended wistfully with wanting him to teach me something useful, like knife sharpening.

Years passed. I showed the poem to a friend. She had never met my grandfather. She had never seen a picture of him, but she wasn't stuck on the oxen, or dazzled by the knives.

"Your grandfather was a man of the earth," she said.

I looked at her wide-eyed and nodded. "He lived life with both hands," I said, by way of agreement.

"Your grandfather's message," she continued, "was that if you slowly increase a challenge it expands ability. He was telling you that youthful exuberance needs to be channeled. Doing the right thing builds strength and character, although it is hard."

I stared at her dumbfounded, as she gathered up my family treasures – the ones I had thrown away in the mud like a fool – and pressed them firmly back into my hand. There was no judgement, and no comment. It was just as if I had accidentally dropped them. But her eyes, oh yes, her eyes made me promise not to lose these gems again, even though we both knew that I had never really owned them in the first place.

Teacher and student. That's the thing. Both need to be present for learning to take place. It is not enough to just learn the words like a parrot, unless years later you hear the words you have been taught and understand. That requires presence, and focus.

You have to live to get that point. Then you'll understand. I'm happy not to be finished with that yet.

ACKNOWLEDGEMENTS

Just as it takes a village to raise a child, it takes an army to publish a book. There are many people I need to thank.

The first person on my list is my amazing wife and best friend, Lisa, who I call "my gift from God." I am so lucky to have her in my life. Although she never met my father, she loves hearing the old stories. She supported me throughout this entire adventure. Lisa not only encouraged me, but listened to the first draft of my stories, and the numerous revisions that followed. She gave me the gift of her ear and has always been my first editor. She was understanding when I had spent the morning writing while other tasks, less important to me, were not completed. Thank you, Lisa, from the bottom of my heart. I could not have done this without your steadfast encouragement support and love. I love you.

The next people I must thank are Harold and Diane Rhenisch. We met at university and have been friends for 40 years. They have listened to me tell fishing stories for decades. Harold, who I have always revered as a mentor, believed my stories were worth telling and there was a book in me somewhere. Both Harold and Diane were cheerleaders and their unwavering friendship and faith in me as a writer was invaluable. This book would not have been possible without them.

I also must thank my father. We had a special relationship and he helped me grow into the man I am now. Even after decades since his passing, I feel his words and guidance with me daily. I will forever be in his debt.

My mother, Crystal Rath, passed away the week I learned this book had been accepted for publication. I was not able to tell her that exciting news, but she was able to hear some of the stories as I read earlier drafts to her. She loved hearing me tell the tales. Perhaps it brought back her own memories of her beloved husband. She was a strong woman and I miss her very much. In my next project, I will tell some of my mother's stories.

I need to also recognize and thank my siblings: Rosemarie Klein, Katharine Howell, and Daniel Rath, who not only shared this journey with me, but provided their unbridled support and encouragement for this book. As an aside, when I told Dan I was working on a book and that I got to be the hero in my own story, I also informed him that he had a part in the story too: he got to be the clown. Without missing a beat, Dan suggested including "clown" in the title. Maybe in the next book, Dan.

A shout out also needs to go to the North Words Writing Conference in Skagway, Alaska, where this book was born at an early morning writing exercise.

There are others, too numerous to name here, that have supported me through this endeavour. Please know your kindness and support has been the fuel I needed to get me through the difficult periods of self-doubt that haunt most writers and helped me realize this goal. Thank you.

And thanks to you the reader, for without readers, my stories would not live on. You make it all worthwhile. I hope you enjoyed the book.

Paul D. Rath is a Canadian who was born in Brazil to Lutheran missionaries Ernest and Crystal Rath. When he was five his parents brought him home to Canada. He has lived in the Peace River country of Northern Alberta, the Okanagan Valley, and Victoria. He currently lives with the catch of his life, his wife Lisa, in the uppermost northwest corner of British Columbia, above Haines, Alaska, where the mountains are many and the people are few.

Rath studied creative writing at the University of Victoria and graduated with a B.A. in 1980. He has worked as a grocer, a letter carrier, a life insurance salesman, and is now retired from the Canada Border Services Agency, which he served in both Osoyoos and as a supervisor in Prince Rupert.

Rath is a contributing writer for *What's Up Yukon*, an arts and entertainment magazine, in which he shares his passion for stories about fishing, community life, and whatever else is happening along the Haines Highway in Alaska, British Columbia, and the Yukon. He is also working on a book of family stories for his grandchildren.

To say Rath is an avid fisherman is a gross understatement. Besides fishing for white fish, kokanee, perch, and trout in the Okanagan Valley, he has caught salmon, halibut, and steelhead on the Pacific North Coast; as well as bluegills and sunfish in the U.S. Paul has caught muskellunge on Lake Sinclair with Detroit visible in the distance; pike (or jackfish) in Alberta, Ontario, and Great Slave Lake; pickerel in Georgian Bay and in Alberta; sailfish off the coast of Costa Rica, while dolphins danced around him; and mahi mahi and barracuda off the coast of the Dominican Republic.

When Rath is not fishing or writing, he is tending to his garden or fussing over his grand composting adventure.

War and Peace with the Beasts

A History of Our Relationships with Animals

Brian Griffith

In this immediately engaging, story- and fact-filled page-turner of a book, Brian Griffith looks at the range of ways we relate to animals and the stories we tell about them. He asks how we choose whether buddyhood, fearful respect, businesslike predation, or genocidal war is the most appropriate response to each species we meet. He watches how our treatment of "inferior beings" affects our treatment of "inferior people," and traces some of the chain reactions we unleash when we try to  weed out species we don't like. "Without much hope of making animals fit my personal preferences," he writes, "I wonder how good our relations can get."

ISBN 978-1-77343-179-6
5" x 8.5" | 216 pages | paperback | $19.95

ALSO AVAILABLE FROM WOOD LAKE

The Architecture of Hope

Douglas MacLeod

Architect and educator Douglas MacLeod offers a stark and immediately compelling glimpse into the future, 15 years hence, in which we can live and work together to build better communities for tomorrow.

This insightful and intriguing book imagines the idea of cooperative communities where people can produce more energy than they use; purify more water than they pollute; grow more food than they consume; and recycle more waste than they produce, with technologies that already exist or that will be within our grasp in a few years.

Most important of all, the people of the community own and profit from these resources.

The Architecture of Hope depicts a way of living that is decentralized, re-localized, and regenerative. And possible.

ISBN 978-1-77343-174-1
4.75" x 7" | 80 pages | paperback | $12.95

Annie Ruth's Truths
Wisdom, Warnings, and Wake-Up Calls

Collected and Written by David Preston Sharp

A humorous, wisdom-filled collection of 111 lively expressions and conversations spoken from the mouth of a remarkable woman, faithfully recorded by her son.

Each of Annie Ruth's sayings is a jewel of language and thought. With explanations where needed, *Annie Ruth's Truths* will make you think, laugh, or shake your head with a smile. And it will wake you up. And that is just what Annie Ruth wants all of us to do – wake up!

Annie Ruth's "truths" cut across culture, race, and nationality, as they contain themes that are part of our common experience as human beings. Young people will benefit from the real world advice, encouragements, and cautions. Older adults will be reminded of sayings from their own particular history, and of the power, faith and wisdom contained in such joy-filled expressions rooted in a Christian aesthetic and a deep love of life. Women will hear Annie Ruth's tough love and feminine strength.

ISBN 978-1-77343-283-0
4.75" x 7" | 128 pages | paperback | $12.95

WOOD LAKE

Publishing Quality Books
Since 1982.

Wood Lake has been telling stories
for more than 35 years.

During that time, it has given form and substance to
the words, songs, pictures, and ideas of hundreds of
authors, artists, and storytellers.

Those stories have taken a multitude of forms – parables,
poems, drawings, prayers, epiphanies, songs, books,
paintings, hymns, and curricula.

Wood Lake honours the enduring art of storytelling
in order to inspire, educate, and connect readers
of every age and culture.

WOOD LAKE PUBLISHING INC.
485 Beaver Lake Road
Kelowna, BC, Canada V4V 1S5
250.766.2778

www.woodlake.com